# Warman's
# PEZ®
## FIELD GUIDE

Shawn Peterson   Edited

**Values and Iden**

©2004 Shawn Peterson

Published by

**krause publications**
An imprint of F+W Publications, Inc.

**700 East State Street • Iola, WI 54990-0001**
**715-445-2214 • 888-457-2873**
**www.krause.com**

Our toll-free number to place an order or obtain
a free catalog is (800) 258-0929.

Library of Congress Catalog Number: 2004093858

ISBN: 0-87349-906-9

Designed by Brian Brogaard

Edited by Tracy L. Schmidt

PEZ® is used throughout this book as a registered trademark.
This book is neither endorsed by, affiliated with, or a product of
Pez Candy Inc.

Printed in the United States of America

# CONTENTS

# INTRODUCTION

Congratulations! You have taken the first step into an exciting, fun hobby that is enjoyed by people from all over the world—collecting PEZ® dispensers! What started out in the 1920s as serious adult product has now become one of the most sought-after collectibles in recent memory. Not only has PEZ® changed to fit the times, it continues to grow and market itself to a whole new generation of collectors. My goal with this book is to show you just how many of those wonderful little dispensers are out there, and how much fun it can be to collect them!

Back in 1990 when I started buying PEZ® at flea markets, I had no idea what was available. I just looked for something I didn't have, and hoped to find a dealer that had boxes full of old dispensers, cheap. While I never found boxes of old PEZ®, I did find many dispensers for under a dollar and my collection started to grow. With each new find proudly displayed on my shelf, I found myself constantly wanting more. One shelf soon lead to several, and now years later those cute little characters have taken over an entire room. I can say one thing for sure, the most fun I have had collecting has come from the people I have met and the friendships made along the way.

Enjoy the journey, have fun collecting!

—*Shawn Peterson*

*All photography was done by Steve Warner.*

# CHAPTER 1
PEZ® HISTORY

The PEZ® dispenser has been around for just over 50 years. PEZ® candy got its start even earlier, introduced in 1927 in Vienna, Austria, as the world's first-ever breath mint. Edward Haas, an avid non-smoker, wanted to invent a product to rival cigarettes. His product, a small compressed sugar tablet with peppermint oil added, was sold in small pocket size tins (similar to Altoid brand mints of today) and marketed as an alternative to smoking. His slogan was "smoking prohibited-pezzing allowed!" But what is "pezzing," or better yet, PEZ®? The name "Pez" was derived from the German word for peppermint, "pfefferminz." Using the first, middle, and last letter of the word, Haas came up with the name "Pez." Twenty years after the candy was invented, in 1948, Oscar Uxa invented and patented a little mechanical box for

dispensing the candy. Resembling a Bic cigarette lighter, the dispenser was marketed as an upscale adult product. The PEZ® "box" had moderate success in Europe, and in 1952 Haas decided to try and conquer the U.S. market. In the span of less than 2 years, he realized that PEZ® was not going to be a worthwhile venture in the United States.

Haas did not give up however, and he decided to reinvent the product by adding fruit flavors to the candy— and a three-dimensional cartoon head to the top of the dispenser. What a success this turned out to be, combining

two of kids' favorite things: candy and a toy! This marketing shift proved to be a brilliant move, making PEZ® one of the most recognizable commercial names around. It is hard to say how many different heads have graced the top of a PEZ® dispenser. Different versions of the same character have been produced and, in some cases, the same version has come in multiple color variations. Conservative estimates put the number between 400-450 different heads.

Despite numerous requests for Elvis and others, PEZ® has never depicted a real person with the exceptions of Betsy Ross, Paul Revere, and Daniel Boone. They have followed this policy for two main reasons: real people rarely have interestingly shaped heads, and the possibility of a real person winding up in a front-page controversy makes the thought less than appealing for a children's product. The company also tries to stay away from passing fads, using only characters that have stood the test of time. At any given time, there are as many as 60-70 different dispensers available at local retailers, not to mention the seasonal ones that appear for such holidays as Christmas, Easter, Halloween, and Valentines Day. PEZ® began offering limited edition dispensers in 1998 with remakes of the classic Psychedelic Hand and Psychedelic Flower. Offered only through the PEZ® Candy Inc. Web site or via phone orders, these limited editions have proven quite popular with collectors.

PEZ®, the company, is divided into two separate entities, PEZ® USA and PEZ® International. PEZ® USA, located in Orange, Connecticut, is responsible for North American distribution, packaging dispensers, and making candy. PEZ® International, now located in Traun, Austria, handles distribution for the rest of the world, along with packaging dispensers and making candy. Although they are separately managed companies, they communicate with each other and sometimes share the cost of producing a new dispenser. The fact that they are two separate companies, and agreements in licensing, account for the reason some dispensers commonly found in the United States are not found anywhere else in the world and vise versa. Depending on how you look at it, this can make collecting more fun or more of a challenge. PEZ® USA is a privately owned business and will not release sales figures to the public, but they do insist that they sell more dispensers per year than there are kids in the United States. Their staff works in three shifts, 24 hours a day, producing the candy and packaging dispensers for shipment all across North America.

The dispenser itself has seen a few modest changes over the years. One of the biggest changes happened in the late 1980s, when "feet" where added to the bottom of the dispenser base to give it more stability when standing upright. Numerous candy and fruit flavors have been produced, ranging from apple to chocolate. Some flavors were more popular than others, and some were just plain strange like chlorophyll, flower, and eucalyptus. Currently the flavors available in the United States are lemon, orange, grape, strawberry, Cola, sour blue raspberry, sour watermelon, sour pineapple, sour green apple, and peppermint.

Although PEZ® has a long history, only recently has it become a hot collectible. PEZ® collecting has been gathering steam since the early 1990s when the first guidebook appeared, depicting all known dispensers and their rarity. The first ever PEZ® convention was held in Mentor, Ohio, on Saturday, June 15, 1991. Several other conventions around the country soon followed. Collectors finally had a chance to meet each other, buy and sell PEZ®, and view rare and unusual dispensers on display. Conventions have quickly become must-attend events for addicted collectors, drawing people from all over the United States and even all over the world.

In 1993, the prestigious Christie's auction house in New York took notice of this evolving hobby and held its first ever pop culture auction featuring PEZ®. The auction realized record prices, taking the hobby to a new level. PEZ® has been featured in countless magazines, TV shows, and news articles—landing on the cover of Forbes magazine in December of 1993. The popular Seinfeld television show even had an episode featuring a Tweety Bird PEZ® dispenser. All this notoriety hasn't gone unnoticed. More and more people have begun to collect these cute character pieces, sending prices into the hundreds and even thousands of dollars for a single dispenser.

PEZ® has done very little in the way of advertising, relying on impulse purchases and parents buying for their kids on a nostalgic whim. While this may not seem like the best marketing method, the company claims it can barely keep up with demand. PEZ® has even become a very popular licensee, with companies vying to put the PEZ® name on everything from clocks to coffee mugs. Hallmark has featured these collectibles on a puzzle and matching greeting card, and has also produced two different PEZ®

dispenser Christmas ornaments.

No one can say for sure where this hobby will go, or if the dispensers will continue to hold their value. In the nearly 15 years that I have been a collector, prices, as well as the collector base, have steadily grown. At present, this hobby has two things in its favor: demand far surpasses the supply of vintage dispensers, and PEZ® is still produced today and can be found in almost any grocery or discount store, making it available to a whole new generation of collectors. With new additions added regularly, the continued success of PEZ® is almost certainly assured.

# CHAPTER 2
## PRICING INFORMATION

A price guide should be viewed as just that—a guide. Since this hobby has become organized, PEZ® prices, like the stock market, have been in nearly constant motion. Prices not only go up, but some DO go down. Several factors account for this fluctuation: supply and demand, emotion, and quantity finds. To pick a point in time and label a dispenser worth exactly "X" amount of dollars, in my opinion, is not in the best interest of the collector. I feel that an average price system is more useful. I have used several sources—online auctions, dealer's lists, and other collectors—to determine what I feel is an accurate price range for each dispenser. Therefore, a price quoted will not reflect the top or bottom dollar that a dispenser has sold for. Dispensers that do not appear for sale often enough to determine an accurate price range will be represented with a price and the "+" symbol.

This pricing information should be used for dispensers that are complete and void of any missing pieces, cracks, chips, or melt marks, and have working spring mechanisms. Dispensers that are broken or missing pieces are not worth nearly as much as complete dispensers. Pricing incomplete or broken dispensers is very subjective. Missing pieces are almost never found. Some collectors don't mind if a dispenser is broken or missing a piece or two, especially if it is a rare dispenser or variation. They may be happy just to have an example in their collection, and hope to upgrade to a dispenser in better condition.

Generally, the value of a dispenser is in the head. Age, country of origin, stem, and patent numbers can also play a part, but are commonly thought of as non-determining factors when assessing the value. Exceptions to this regarding the stems are features such as die-cuts, advertising, or pictures, such as found on the witch regular. One or more of these features can actually increase the value of the dispenser. Other stem characteristics must be present in certain dispensers to complete the value and be considered correct. For example, the football player stem will have one smooth side with an upside down pennant-shaped triangle molded in. Also, all of the original psychedelics will have at least one, and sometimes two, smooth sides to which a sticker was applied (stickers must still be intact). Swirled or marbleized stems can also add value to a dispenser. Some collectors are willing to pay a bit more for these as they can be very difficult to find and no two are exactly alike. Finally, resale is something you may want to consider. A complete, mint condition dispenser will always be easier to sell than one that has problems or is missing parts.

### A Word of Caution

Collectors beware: Some people have begun making and selling reproduction parts for PEZ®. Some are better skilled at this than others. Trust your instinct. If you think an item is questionable, it is better to pass than find out later that you have been taken. Know what you are buying and be familiar with what a piece should look like.

Some dispensers, such as Elvis and KISS, were never made by PEZ® but can be found with relative ease. How can this be? When a dispenser of a certain character or person is in demand but does not exist, collectors have sometimes resorted to making their own dispensers. These are known as "fan-made" or "fantasy" pieces. Again, some of these pieces are better made than others; in fact, some are quite good. You can even find fantasy pieces that are mint on a very convincing PEZ® card, but in reality never existed. Most of these dispensers sell in the $25 or less range and are considered by some to be very collectable.

Only knowledge, experience, and buying from a well known, reputable dealer will help avoid having a reproduction or fake unknowingly passed on to you. Common reproduction parts include but are not limited to: the ringmaster's moustache, the Mexican's goatee and earrings, the policeman's and fireman's hat badges, the knight's plume, the doctor's reflector, and Batman's cape. Most parts are not labeled as reproductions. For instance, a remake of the doctor's reflector is made of aluminum instead of plastic, and the reproduction capes for Batman are usually much thicker than the vintage capes. Studying pictures in books and going to PEZ® conventions are your best sources for comparing dispensers. A great deal of information can also be found on the Internet. There are many PEZ®-related Web sites made by collectors that will answer almost any question related to the hobby.

# CHAPTER 3
## How to Use this Guide

The dispensers are listed in alphabetical order. The common name of the dispenser is listed first, followed by any alternate names. Next you will find a date—this is when production of the dispenser started. Notes on whether the dispenser was made with or without feet (or both) are also included. Finally, a value will be given for the dispenser as well as for known variations.

Values given are for loose dispensers complete with all working parts, and have no melt marks, cracks, or chips. Pricing packaged dispensers is a bit more subjective. Some collectors have little or no interest in packaged dispensers, as they want to display their collections more creatively. Currently, there is little interest in poly bag packaging. Clear cello bags may add a little value to a dispenser. For example, if the dispenser is worth $50, it might bring $55-$60 if packaged in a clear cello bag. The exceptions to this are dispensers that are packaged with an insert, sticker, comic, advertising, or a rare pack of candy. Sometimes these inserts are worth more than the dispenser. Dispensers mounted on cards are considered the most desirable of packaged dispensers. Factors affecting the value of a carded dispenser are condition of the card, and graphics or artwork on the card. Seasonal cards with neat artwork are worth more than plain, solid-color cards.

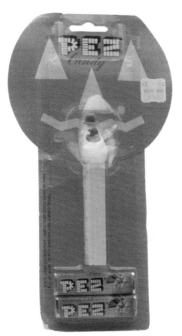

*Clown with chin on a rare die-cut Halloween card. $200-$250*

*1980s silver space gun.* **$100-$150**

*1980s red space gun.* **$85-$125**

### 1980s Space Gun
PEZ® produced another space gun in the 1980s to capitalize on the space craze caused by the *Star Wars* movies. Two versions exist, a Hong Kong version and an Austrian version.

**Silver Space Gun:** . . . . . . . . . $100-$150
**Red Space Gun:** . . . . . . . . . . $85-$125

*Admiral. A very rare dispenser, this is the only one currently known to exist.* **$3000+**

## Admiral

Date Unknown, no feet

A very rare dispenser, this is the only one currently known to exist. The Admiral character has been shown on various PEZ® advertisements such as comics and candy boxes, but none had been found until early 2000.

**Value:** . . . . . . . . . . . . . . . . . **$3000+**

*Alpine Man, from the 1972
Munich Olympics.* **$1500+**
*(From the Maryann Kennedy
collection.)*

## Alpine Man
Early 1970s, no feet
Produced for the 1972 Munich Olympics, this is a very rare and
difficult dispenser to find.
**Value: . . . . . . . . . . . . . . . . . . $1500+**

*Three versions of the Angel dispenser.* **(L to R)** *Yellow hair with feet* **$50-$65**, *yellow hair without feet* **$85-$100**, *and a rare blonde version.* **$90-$125**

## Angel

Early 1970s, no feet and with feet
Several versions of the Angel have been produced, including one with a small plastic loop on the back of her hair that allows it to be used as an ornament.

No feet: . . . . . . . . . . . . . . . . $85-$100
With feet: . . . . . . . . . . . . . . . $50-$65
Unusual blond hair version: . . . $90-$125
Ornament: . . . . . . . . . . . . . . . $100-$125

*Angel with removable eyes and larger than normal halo.* **$85-$100**

*Unusual version of Angel with loop.*
**$100-$125**
*(From the Johann Patek collection.)*

### Annie
Early 1980s, no feet
Released to coincide with the release of the
movie *Annie*. The movie wasn't a hit and
neither was the dispenser, making this one
a little tough to find.
**Value:** ................... **$150-$175**

*Annie, released during the early 1980s around the
movie* Annie. **$150-$175**

## Arithmetic Dispensers

Early 1960s

Arithmetic Regulars were available as a mail-in premium as well as sold in stores. They can be found in red, blue, green, tan, and yellow.

Blue: . . . . . . . . . . . . . . . . . . . $500-$700
Green: . . . . . . . . . . . . . . . . . . $600-$800
Red: . . . . . . . . . . . . . . . . . . . $700-$900
Tan or yellow: . . . . . . . . . . . . $800-$1000

*Arithmetic dispenser, blue version.* **$500-$700**

*Arithmetic dispenser insert.*

## Asterix

Asterix is a popular European comic. These dispensers have not been released in the U.S. The series was first produced by PEZ® in the mid-1970s and a remake of the original series was released in the late 1990s. The remakes have feet and painted-on eyes. The Roman Soldier was not included in the original series.

## Asterix

Mid-1970s, no feet and with feet
**Original:** . . . . . . . . . . . . . . . **$1500-$2000**
**Remake:** . . . . . . . . . . . . . . . **$3-$5**

## Muselix

Mid-1970s, no feet and with feet
**Original:** . . . . . . . . . . . . . . . **$2500-$3000**
**Remake, called 'Getafix' by PEZ: $3-$5**

*Original Asterix from the mid-1970s.*
***$1500-$2000***
*(From the Maryann Kennedy collection.)*

## Obelix

Mid-1970s, no feet and with feet
**Original:** . . . . . . . . . . . . . . . **$1500-$2000**
**Remake:** . . . . . . . . . . . . . . . **$3-$5**

## Roman Soldier

Late 1990s, with feet
**Value:** . . . . . . . . . . . . . . . . . **$3-$5**

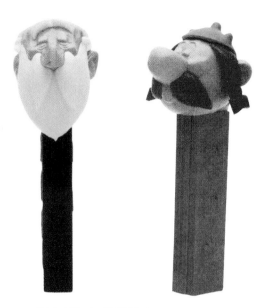

*Original Muselix* **(L)** **$2500-$3000** *and Obelix* **(R).**
**$1500-$2000**
*(Obelix is from the Maryann Kennedy collection.)*

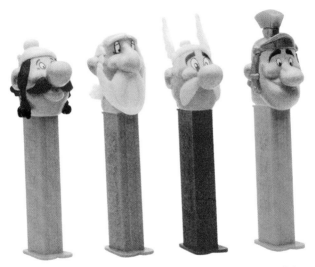

*Remake of the Asterix series.* **(L to R)** *Obelix, Muselix (sometimes called "Getafix"), Asterix, and Roman Soldier.* **$3-$5**

## Astronaut

Early 1960s, no feet

The Astronaut 1 was not released in the U.S., but the second Astronaut, released in the 1970s, was distributed in the U.S. A very rare version of this dispenser exists and is known as the "World's Fair Astronaut" because of the inscription on the left side of the stem. Only two of these dispensers are known to exist—one with a green stem and white helmet and the other with a blue-green stem and matching helmet.

Astronaut 1: . . . . . . . . . . . . . . $600-$700
Astronaut 2 white helmet/green stem: $125-$150
Astronaut 2 blue helmet/blue stem: . . $140-$160
World's Fair Astronaut: . . . . . . $3000+

*Astronaut 1, from the early 1960s. This dispenser was not released in the U.S., and can also be found with a white or light blue helmet.*
**$600-$700**

*Astronaut 2 from the late 1970s. White helmet/green stem*
**$125-$150**, *blue helmet/stem.* **$140-$160**

## Baloo
Late 1960s, no feet and with feet
Although difficult to find, Baloo was also
produced with a yellow or red head.
**Blue-gray head, no feet: . . . . . $30-$40**
**Blue-gray head, with feet: . . . . $20-$30**
**Red or Yellow head, no feet: . . $300+**

*Baloo from the Jungle Book series, released in the
late 1960s.* **$30-$40**

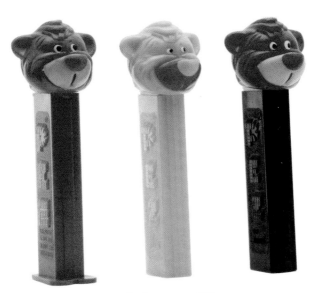

*Unusual Baloo variations.* **$300+**
*(From the Johann Patek collection.)*

## Bambi

Late 1970s, no feet and with feet
The same mold was used for the Rudolph dispenser but with a black nose. A rare version of this dispenser, although subtle, carries the copyright symbol along with the letters "WDP" on the head, which can at least double the value.

**No copyright, no feet:** . . . . . . . $45-$60
**No copyright, with feet:** . . . . . . $35-$45
**With copyright, no feet:** . . . . . $125-$150

*Bambi, from the late 1970s. The same mold was used to make the Rudolph dispenser.* **$85-$100**

**Barney Bear**

Early 1980s, no feet and with feet

**No feet:** . . . . . . . . . . . . . . . . . **$35-$45**
**With feet:** . . . . . . . . . . . . . . . **$20-$30**

*Barney Bear, an MGM character released in the early 1980s, yellow stem and feet.* **$20-$30**

*Barney Bear, with red stem and feet.*
**$20-$30**

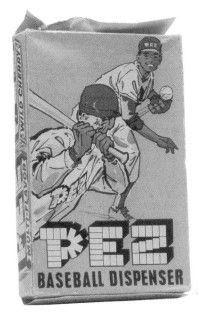

*Backside of rare vending box. (From the Maryann Kennedy collection.)*

## Baseball Set

Mid-1960s, no feet

This set consisted of a dispenser with a baseball mitt "head" and a removable ball, bat, and home plate. It is difficult to find with the bat and home plate. The vending box is also very rare, as only a few examples are known to have survived.

**Value:** . . . . . . . . . . . . . . . . . **$600-$800**

*Baseball set from the mid-1960s with rare vending box.*
**$600-$800**
*(From the Maryann Kennedy collection.)*

## Batman

Late 1960s, no feet and with feet
Batman has gone through several
different looks and can still be found
today. Batman with cape is the earliest
version and collectors should be aware
that reproductions of the cape have been
made. The original cape can be somewhat
translucent whereas reproduction capes
are much thicker.

**Batman with cape:** ......... $75-$120
**Short ears, no feet:** ........ $20-$30
**Short ears, with feet:** ...... $10-$15
**Short ears, with feet, black**
**(available for a very short time in the mid-
1990s):** .................. $10-$15

*Rare green Batman test mold.* **$NA**
*(From the Johann Patek collection.)*

*Batman, Dark Knight (**L to R**) pointy ear version $3-$6, and rounded ear version $1-$2.*

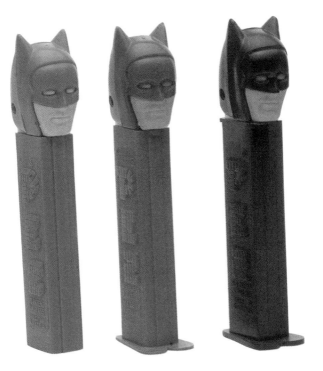

(L to R) *1960s Batman, no feet* **$20-$30**, *with feet* **$10-$15**, *and mid-1990s black short ears.* **$10-$15**

*Unusual color variations of the late 1990s bear.*
**$5-$10**

## Bear

Late 1990s, with feet
This dispenser uses the same head as the Icee Bear and the FAO Schwarz Bear, and is not available in the U.S.
**Value:** . . . . . . . . . . . . . . . . . . **$5-$10**

## Betsy Ross
Mid-1970s, no feet
**Value:** . . . . . . . . . . . . . . . . . **$125-$150**

*Betsy Ross from the 1975 Bicentennial series.*
*$125-$150*

### Bob the Builder
2002, with feet
**Value:** . . . . . . . . . . . . . . . . . **$2-$4**

*Bob from the 2002 Bob the Builder series.*
**$2-$4**

*Wendy, Pritchard the Cat, and Spud the Scarecrow from the
Bob the Builder series.*
**$2-$4**

## Boy and Boy with Cap

Mid-1960s to current, no feet and with feet
Many versions of the PEZ® Pal Boy have
been produced through the years. One of
the rarest is the brown-hair boy without hat
used in a mid-1980s promotion for the movie
*Stand By Me.* The dispenser is packaged
with one pack of multi-flavor candy and
a miniature version of the movie poster
announcing the videocassette release and the
quote, "If I could only have one food to eat
for the rest of my life? That's easy, PEZ®.
Cherry flavored PEZ®. No question about
it." This dispenser must be sealed in original
bag to be considered complete.

**Boy with blue cap, blond hair:** . $100-$125
**Boy with red cap, blond hair:** . . $250-$300
**Boy with blue cap, brown hair:** $75-$100
**Blond hair:** . . . . . . . . . . . . . $50-$75
**Brown hair:** . . . . . . . . . . . . . $25-$35
**Stand By Me (sealed in bag
with mini-poster):** . . . . . . . . $200-$250

*Boy with blond hair.* **$50-$75**

*Boy with Cap (blue) and blond hair.*
**$100-$125**

*Boy with brown hair.*
**$25-$35**

*Boy with Cap (blue) and brown hair.*
**$75-$100**

## Bozo the Clown

Early 1960s, no feet
This dispenser is usually die-cut on the side of the stem with a picture of Bozo and Butch. The non-die-cut stem is actually more difficult to find.

**Die-cut stem:** . . . . . . . . . . . . . $175-$200
**Plain stem:** . . . . . . . . . . . . . $185-$200

*Bozo the Clown plain stem.* **$185-$225**

*Limited Edition Bride and Groom.* $30-$45 *per set*

## Bride and Groom (LIMITED EDITION)
Current, with feet
Limited edition Bride and Groom dispensers (mail order only).

**Value:** . . . . . . . . . . . . . . . . . . $30-$45 per set
**African American**
**variation (2004)** . . . . . . . . . . $25-$35 per set

*The rare and much-desired Bride, orange hair.* **$1800-$2000**

## Bride

Late 1970s, no feet
The Bride is a very rare and much desired piece by collectors.
This dispenser, along with the Groom, was created for Robert and
Claudia's wedding (relatives of a PEZ® executive) that took place
October 6, 1978. They were used as place setting gifts and each
guest received a set. The Bride is much harder to find than the
Groom. It should be noted that the hair is different than the hair on
the nurse.

**Orange hair:**  . . . . . . . . . . . . $1800-$2000
**Brown hair:**  . . . . . . . . . . . . . $2000-$2200
**Blonde hair:**  . . . . . . . . . . . . $2100-$2300

## Bubbleman

Mid-1990s, with feet
This dispenser was only available from PEZ®
through a mail-in offer. The Bubbleman was
the first set offered in this manner. They have
the copyright date of 1992 on the dispenser,
but didn't appear until the fall of 1996.

Value: . . . . . . . . . . . . . . . . . . $5-$10 each
Neon Bubbleman (1998): . . . . . $3-$6 each
Crystal Bubbleman (1999): . . . $3-$6 each
Glowlng Bubbleman: . . . . . . . . $3-$6 each

*Example of Crystal Bubbleman.* $3-$6

*Crystal Bubbleman assortment.* **$3-$6**

*Glowing Bubbleman. Available through mail order only.* **$3-$6**

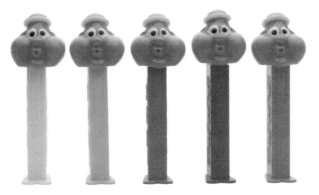

*Original Bubbleman dispensers.* **$5-$10**

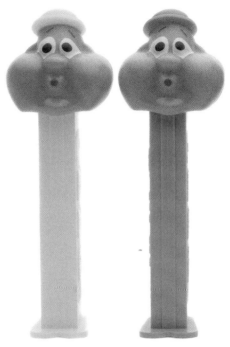

*Neon Bubbleman dispensers.* **$3-$6**

*Additional examples of the Neon Bubbleman dispensers.*

## Bugs Bunny
Late 1970s to current, no feet and with feet

**No feet:** . . . . . . . . . . . . . . . . . $15-$20
**With feet, older-style head:** . . . $5-$10
**Painted ears:** . . . . . . . . . . . . . $1-$2
**Current:** . . . . . . . . . . . . . . . . $1-$2

*Current Bugs Bunny dispenser.* **$1-$2**

*Bugs Bunny dispensers from the late 1970s* **(L to R)**, *no feet* **$15-$20**, *with feet (2 examples)* **$5-$10**, *and painted ears.* **$1-$2**

### Bugz

Summer, 2000 with feet
The PEZ® Web site calls them Barney
Beetle, Jumpin' Jack the grasshopper,
Florence Flutterfly, Sam Snuffle the fly,
Super Bee, Sweet Ladybird the ladybug, the
clumsy worm, and good-natured centipede.
The Crystal Bugz pictured on pages 61-67
are special ones found only through mail
order or Wal Mart Kids' connection candy
stores.

**Value:** . . . . . . . . . . . . . . . . . **$1-$2 each**
**Crystal Bugz:** . . . . . . . . . . . . **$4-$6 each**

*Caterpillar.* **$1-$2**

*Sweet Ladybird* **$1-$2**, *Crystal Sweet Ladybird* **$4-$6**, *Clumsy Worm* **$1-$2**, *and Crystal Clumsy Worm.* **$4-$6**

*The "smart bee" or baby bee, regular* **$1-$2**, *crystal.* **$4-$6**

*Caterpillar* **(L)** **$1-$2**, *and Crystal Caterpillar* **(R)**. **$4-$6**

*Beetle* **(L)**, *Grasshopper* **$1-$2**, *and Crystal Grasshopper.* **$4-$6**

*Flutterfly, regular* **(R)** *$1-$2, and crystal* **(L).** *$4-$6*

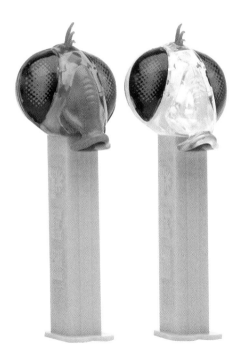

*Fly, regular* **(L)** *$1-$2, and crystal* **(R)**. *$4-$6*

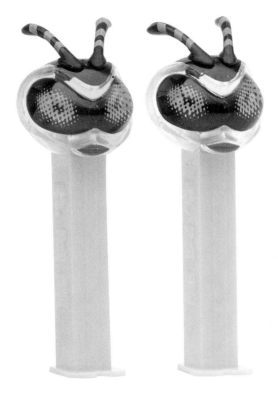

*Bee, regular* **(L)** **$1-$2**, *and crystal* **(R)**. **$4-$6**

*Beetle* **(L)** *and Grasshopper.* **$1-$2**

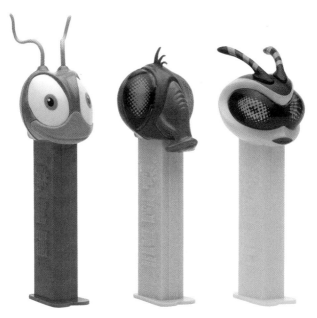

*Flutterfly* **(L)***, Fly, and Bee.* **$1-$2**

### Bullwinkle
Early 1960s, no feet
Bullwinkle can be found with either a
yellow or a brown stem—the brown is
much harder to find.

**Yellow stem:** .............. **$250-$275**
**Brown stem:** .............. **$275-$325**

*Bullwinkle, yellow stem.* **$250-$275**

*Bullwinkle, brown stem.* **$275-$325**

## Camel (whistle)

No feet and with feet
The camel can be found with either a
brown or a tan head.

**No feet:** . . . . . . . . . . . . . . . . . **$60-$75**
**With feet:** . . . . . . . . . . . . . . **$40-$60**

*Camel, whistle with feet.* **$40-$60**

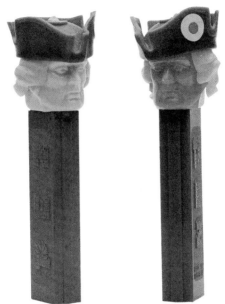

*Captain, also known as Paul Revere. He should have the sticker on the left side of his hat to be complete.* **$150-$175**

## Captain (Also known as Paul Revere)

Mid-1970s, no feet

This dispenser should have a sticker on the left side of his hat to be considered complete.

**Value: . . . . . . . . . . . . . . . . . $150-$175**

*Captain America, black mask version* **(L)** **$100-$125**,
*blue mask version* **(R)**. **$85-$110**

## Captain America

Late 1970s, no feet
Captain America was produced with a black and a blue mask—the
black mask is tougher to find.

**Black mask:** . . . . . . . . . . . . . **$100-$125**
**Blue mask:** . . . . . . . . . . . . . **$85-$110**

## Captain Hook
Late 1960s, no feet
A very rare softhead version of this
dispenser was produced in the late 1970s,
but never went into general production.
Value: . . . . . . . . . . . . . . . . . . $100-$140
Softhead: . . . . . . . . . . . . . . $3000+

*Captain Hook.* **$100-$140**

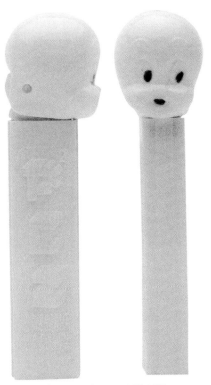

*Casper, regular stem.* **$150-$175**

## Casper

Late 1950s, no feet

No one is sure which licensed character first graced the top of a PEZ® dispenser. Some say it was Mickey Mouse, some say Popeye, and others say Casper. One story has it that Curt Allina, executive vice-president of PEZ® from 1953 to 1979, and Mr. Harvey, creator of Casper, had apartments in the same New York building in the 1950s. While living there the two developed a friendship and an agreement to use Harvey's character on the candy dispenser. The rest, as they say, is history.

Casper can be found with white, light blue, and light yellow stems as well as a die-cut version with a red or black sleeve.

**Value:** . . . . . . . . . . . . . . . . . . **$150-$175**
**Die-cut stem:** . . . . . . . . . . . . **$200-$250**

## Cat with Derby (also known as Puzzy Cat)
Early 1970s, no feet
Several head and hat color combinations are available, as are many stem colors. The blue hat version is the rarest, selling for twice that of other versions.

**Value:** . . . . . . . . . . . . . . . . . . **$85-$95**
**Blue hat:** . . . . . . . . . . . . . . . **$150-$175**

*Cat with Derby.* **$85-$95**

*Cat with Derby,* **(L)** *and* **(R)** *versions* **$85-$95,**
*blue hat version* **(C).** **$150-$175**

## Chick in Egg

Early 1970s to current, no feet and with feet
The earliest versions of this popular
dispenser have a brittle plastic eggshell
with jagged points. The second version
has a thin, flexible plastic shell with more
uniform points that resemble a saw blade.
The third version, from the 1980s, has a
much thicker shell, but with the same type
of points as on the second version. The
current version is also a thicker plastic, but
there are fewer points on the shell and edges
are more rounded.

**Chick in Egg, no hat, no feet:** . . $85-$120
**Chick in Egg A,**
**with hat, no feet:** . . . . . . . . . . . $75-$100
**Chick in Egg B,**
**with hat, no feet:** . . . . . . . . . . . $15-$25
**Chick in Egg B,**
**with feet:** . . . . . . . . . . . . . . . $2-$4
**Chick in Egg C,**
**with hat, no feet:** . . . . . . . . . . . $10-$15
**Chick in Egg C,**
**with hat, with feet:** . . . . . . . . . $5-$10
**Chick in Egg D,**
**with hat, with feet:** . . . . . . . . . . $2-$3
**Chick in Egg E,**
**with hat, with feet (current):** . . . $1-$2

*Chick in Egg A, with hat, old version with thin, brittle*
*shell. Notice the steel pin.* **$75-$100**

*Chick in Egg A, no hat, the oldest version.* **$85-$120**

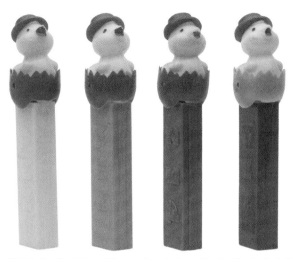

*Chick in Egg B, with hat. This second version has a thin, flexible plastic shell with more uniform points that resemble a saw blade.* **$15 $25**

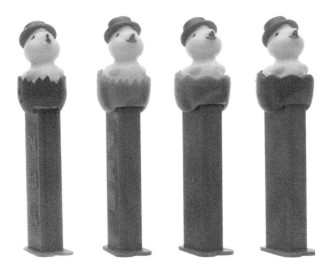

*More recent versions of the Chick in Egg with hat from the 1980s to current. The dispenser on the far left is version B with feet **$2-$4**, version C with feet is next to that **$5-$10**, and the two on the right are version D with feet. **$2-$3***

*Three variations of the Chick in Egg, without hat.* **$85-$120**
*(From the Johann Patek collection.)*

*Chick on Easter card.* **$150-$200** *(From the Maryann Kennedy collection.)*

## Chip

Late 1970s, no feet and with feet
PEZ® only produced one half of the
famous Disney chipmunk duo of Chip and
Dale.

**No feet:** . . . . . . . . . . . . . . . . . $75-$100
**With feet:** . . . . . . . . . . . . . . $50-$75

*Chip, with feet.* **$50-$75**

*Chip, no feet.* **$75-$100**

## Clown with Chin (Also known as Long Face Clown)
Mid-1970s, no feet
This dispenser can be found with many hair, hat, and nose color combinations.
**Value:** . . . . . . . . . . . . . . . . . **$85-$100**

*Clown with Chin.* **$85-$100**

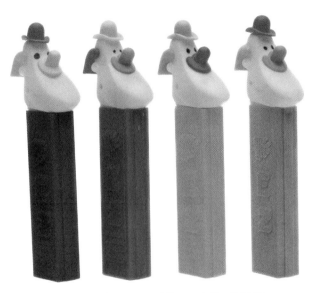

*Additional color variations of Clown with Chin.* **$85-$100**

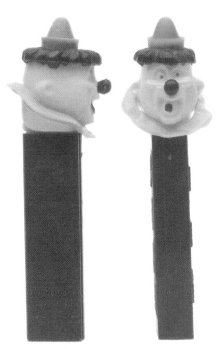

*Clown with Collar.* **$60-$75**

## Clown with Collar
1960s, no feet
**Value:** . . . . . . . . . . . . . . . . . . **$60-$75**

### Clown (whistle)
No feet and with feet
**No feet:** .................. $12-$15
**With feet:** ............... $5-$10

*Clown, whistle with feet.* $5-$10

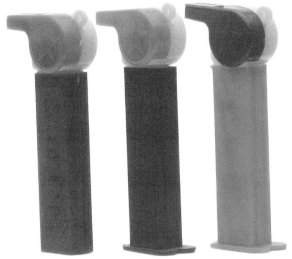

*Coach's Whistle, no feet* **(L)** *$35-$50, and with feet* **(R).** *$1-$3*

## Coach's Whistle
No feet and with feet

**No feet:** . . . . . . . . . . . . . . . . . $35-$50
**With feet:** . . . . . . . . . . . . . . . $1-$3

*Coach's Whistle, with feet.* **$1-$3**

## Cockatoo

Mid-1970s, no feet and with feet
Several head and beak color combinations are available. The peach-colored beak is harder to find and worth significantly more than other colors.

No feet: . . . . . . . . . . . . . . . . . $65-$85
With feet:. . . . . . . . . . . . . . . $45-$65

*Cockatoo, no feet.* **$65-$85**

*Additional color variations of Cockatoo no feet.* **$65-$85**

*Cool Cat, with feet.* **$45-$65**

# Cool Cat
Early 1980s, no feet and with feet
**No feet:** . . . . . . . . . . . . . . . . . . **$65-$85**
**With feet:** . . . . . . . . . . . . . . **$45-$65**

*Cow A. The rare green head version (L) sells for two to three times as much as the blue version (R). $100-$125 (Green head from the Maryann Kennedy collection.)*

## Cow A
Early 1970s, no feet
There are many different color variations of the head. The green head is a rare variation and sells for two to three times as much as other versions.

**Value:** ................. **$100-$125**

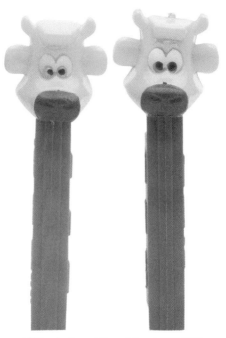

*Additional color variations of Cow A.* **$100-$125**

*There are many color variations of the Cow A head.* **$100-$125**

*Cow A, rare brown variation.* **$NA**
*(From the Johann Patek collection.)*

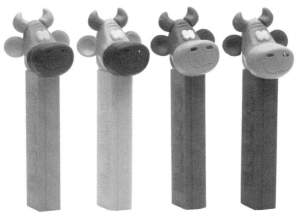

*Many color combinations can be found of the Cow B dispenser. $85-$120
(Green and yellow cow from the Maryann Kennedy collection.)*

## Cow B
Mid-1970s, no feet
Many different color combinations can be found. The same mold was used to make the head for the Yappy Dog.
**Value: . . . . . . . . . . . . . . . . . $85-$120**

*Cowboy.* **$200-$250**

**Cowboy**
Early 1970s, no feet
**Value:** . . . . . . . . . . . . . . . . . . **$200-$250**

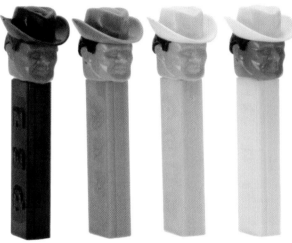

*Cowboy variations.* **$200-$250**
*(From the Johann Patek collection.)*

### Crazy Animals
Released fall 1999, with feet
Not sold in the U.S.
Four animals: Frog, Shark, Octopus, and
Camel.
**Value: . . . . . . . . . . . . . . . . . . $1-$3**

*Crazy Animals Frog.* **$1-$3**

*Crazy Animals Shark, Octopus, and Camel.* **$1-$3**

## Crazy Fruit Series
Mid-1970s, no feet
The Orange first appeared in the mid-1970s,
followed by the Pear and Pineapple in the late
1970s. The Pineapple is the hardest of the
three to find, followed by the Pear, then the
Orange. The Lemon was made as a production
sample, but never produced.

Orange: . . . . . . . . . . . . . . . . . $200-$250
Pear: . . . . . . . . . . . . . . . . . $800-$1000
Pineapple: . . . . . . . . . . . . . $2500-$3000
Lemon: . . . . . . . . . . . . . . . . . $3000+

*The ultra-rare Lemon Crazy Fruit dispenser—this is a
production sample; the dispenser was never produced.*
**$3000+**
*(From the Dora Dwyer collection.)*

*Crazy Fruit series* **(L to R)** *Pear* **$800-$1000**, *Orange* **$200-$250**, *and Pineapple.*
**$2500-$3000**
*(Pear and Pineapple from the Maryann Kennedy collection.)*

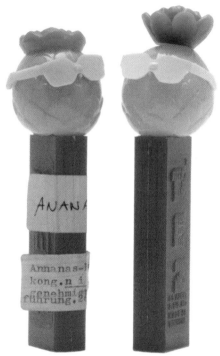

*Ultra-rare short stem Pineapple* **(L)** *$NA, and regular version* **(R)**.
**$2500-$3000**
*(From the Johann Patek collection.)*

*Crazy Fruit series Pear* **$800-$1000**, *and Orange.* **$200-$250**

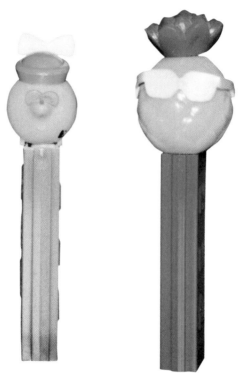

*Crazy Fruit series Lemon* **(L)** $3000+, *and Pineapple* **(R).** $2500-$3000
*(From the Dora Dwyer collection.)*

### Crocodile
Mid-1970s, no feet
Can be found in several shades of green
and even in purple. The purple version
sells for about twice as much as green
dispensers.
**Value (green head crocodiles):**
. . . . . . . . . . . . . . . . . . . . . . **$100-$125**

*Crocodile, green head.* **$100-$125**

## Crystal Ball Dispenser

Sold through a 2002 mail-in offer for
$15.95. It has tiny silver sparkles in
the stem and base. The first 2500 were
made by mistake using silver stars, the
remaining production will have blue
stars.

**Value:** . . . . . . . . . . . . . . . . . **$15.95**

*Crystal Ball Dispenser, with silver stars.* **$15.95**

*Crystal Ball Dispenser, with blue stars.* **$15.95**

## Crystal Dinosaur
1999, with feet
Only available through PEZ® mail-in offer.
**Value:** . . . . . . . . . . . . . . . . . . **$3-$5**

*Crystal Dinosaur.* $3-$5

*Additional Crystal Dinosaurs.* **$3-$5**

## Daffy Duck

Late 1970s to current, no feet and with feet
Many versions of Daffy have been produced.
The first version with separate eye pieces is the
toughest to find.

**Daffy Duck A** (separate eye pieces): . $25-$30
**Daffy Duck B** (painted eyes and tongue): $15-$20
**Daffy Duck C** (with feet, older-style head): $5-$8
**Daffy Duck D** (current style): . . . . . $1-$2

*Current Daffy Duck.* $1-$2

*Daffy Duck grouping, (L) version is the toughest to find with separate eye pieces and is valued at $25-$30.*

**Daisy Duck**
Late 1990s, with feet
**Value:** .................. **$1-$2**

*Daisy Duck.* **$1-$2**

## Dalmatian Pup
Late 1970s, no feet and with feet
**No feet:** . . . . . . . . . . . . . . . . . **$75-$95**
**With feet:** . . . . . . . . . . . . . . . **$60-$75**

*Dalmatian Pup, with feet.* **$60-$75**

## Daniel Boone
Mid-1970s, no feet

**Value:** ................... **$175-$200**

*Daniel Boone, no feet.* **$175-$200**

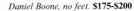

## Die-Cuts
Early 1960s

A Die-Cut dispenser is one in which a design is cut into the side of the stem. The cutout usually reveals an inner sleeve of a different color. Several dispensers were made with a die-cut stem in the 1960s.

**Casper:** .................. $250-$275
**Donald Duck:** ............. $175-$200
**Mickey Mouse:** ........... $125-$175
**Easter Rabbit:** ........... $500-$600
**Bozo:** ................... $175-$200

*Bozo, Die-cut dispenser.* **$175-$200**

*Mickey Mouse* **(L)** *$125-$175, and Easter Bunny*
**(R)** *die-cut dispenser.* **$500-$600**

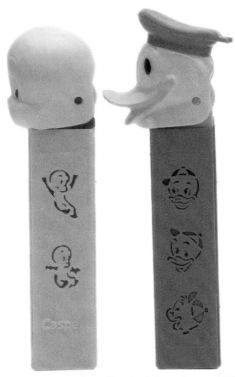

*Casper* **(L)** $250-$275, *and Donald Duck* **(R)** *die-cut dispenser.* **$175-$200**

## Dinosaurs

Early 1990s, with feet

The dinosaurs were first released in Europe in the early 1990s and were known as the "Trias Family"—Brutus, Titus, Chaos, and Venesia. Shortly thereafter, they were introduced to the United States as "Pez-a-Saurs."

**Value:** . . . . . . . . . . . . . . . . . . **$1-$2**

*She-Saur dinosaur.* **$1-$2**

*Fly-Saur dinosaur.* **$1-$2**

*He-Saur* **(L)** *and L-Saur* **(R).** **$1-$2**

## Disney Softheads
Late 1970s
These dispensers are ultra rare and were never sold to the public. The few that are known to exist have come from former employees of PEZ®. There are six dispensers in this group: Pluto, Donald Duck, Goofy, Captain Hook, Dumbo, and Mickey Mouse.

**Value:** . . . . . . . . . . . . . . . . . **$3000+ each**

*Disney Softheads were never put on stems. The ones shown here are for display purposes only.*
*Dumbo Softhead. $3000+*
*(From the Dora Dwyer collection.)*

*Goofy, Donald, and Captain Hook Softheads.* **$3000+**
*(From the Dora Dwyer collection.)*

*Mickey Mouse, Pluto, and Goofy Softheads.* **$3000+**
*(From the Dora Dwyer collection.)*

*Disney Softheads. Ultra rare and never sold to the public. Shown are Goofy, Donald, and Pluto.* **$3000+ ea.**
*(From the Maryann Kennedy collection.)*

### Doctor and Nurse
Early 1970s, no feet
Both of these dispensers are available in several versions. The doctor comes with OR without hair on either a blue, white, or yellow stem. The nurse can be found with brown, reddish orange, yellow, or blonde hair on several different stem colors. There is also a variation in her hat: one is a solid white and the other is an opaque or milky-white, semi-transparent color that is usually only found in dispensers that came from Canada.

**Doctor with hair:** . . . . . . . . . . $150-$250
**Doctor without hair** . . . . . . . . $100-$125
**Nurse:** . . . . . . . . . . . . . . . . $150-$200

*Nurse with reddish-orange hair.* **$150-$200**

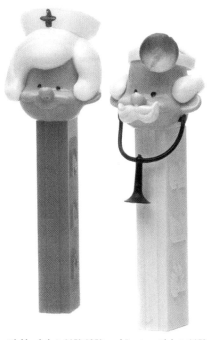

*Nurse with blonde hair* **$150-$250**, *and Doctor with hair.* **$150-$200**

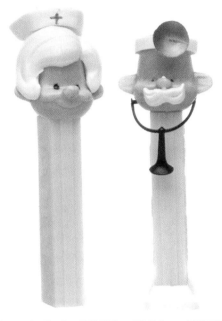

*Nurse with yellow hair* **$150-$250**, *and Bald Doctor.* **$100-$125**

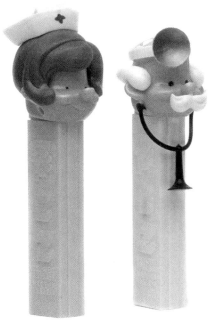

*Nurse with brown hair* **$150-$250**, *and Doctor with hair.* **$150-$200**

### Dog (whistle)
No feet and with feet

**No feet:** . . . . . . . . . . . . . . . . . . $30-$40
**With feet:** . . . . . . . . . . . . . . . $20-$30

*Dog, whistle, no feet.* **$30-$40**

## Donald Duck

Early 1960s to current, no feet and with feet
Many versions of Donald have been made over
the years. Version D, which has holes in the beak,
was also used as the head of the Uncle Scrooge
McDuck dispenser. An extemely rare "softhead"
version also exists, but these never made it to
general production.

**Version A, (original-early 1960s) sharp, defined
feathers, no feet: . . . . . . . . . . $20-$30**
**Version B, a remake of A with the feathers less
defined on top of head, no feet:  $15-$25**
**Version C, 2 hinge-holes on the side of the head,
milky white plastic head, early-mid-1970s, no feet
and with feet:  . . . . . . . . . . . $15-$25**

*Donald Duck, version E with light eyes.* **$2-$4**

*Donald Duck, version
E with dark blue eyes
(L), and version F
(R). $1-$2*

Version D, 2 hinge-holes on the side of the head, hole in beak, no feet
and with feet: . . . . . . . . . . . . $10-$20
Version E, produced in the 1980s, came with both light and dark blue
eyes:. . . . . . . . . . . . . . . . . . . $2-$4
Version F, late 1990s version, the
beak is open: . . . . . . . . . . . . . $1-$2
Softhead version: . . . . . . . . . $3000+

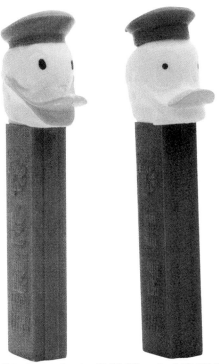

*Donald Duck, original version* **(L)** **$20-$30**, *version B* **(R).** **$15-$25**

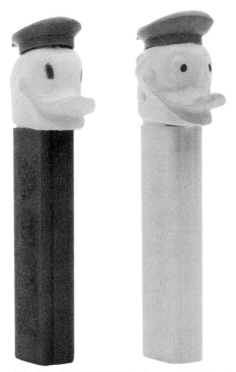

*Donald Duck, version C* **(L)** *$15-$25, and version B* **(R).** **$15-$25**

### Donkey (whistle)
No feet and with feet

**No feet:** . . . . . . . . . . . . . . . . . $35-$45
**With feet:** . . . . . . . . . . . . . . . $5-$10

*Donkey, whistle with feet.* **$5-$10**

**Dopey**
Late 1960s, no feet
**Value:** . . . . . . . . . . . . . . . . . $200-$225

*Dopey.* **$200-$225**

## Droopy

Early 1980s, no feet and with feet
This dispenser was not released in the U.S. Two
versions were made—one with painted ears and
one with movable ears.

**Painted ears:** . . . . . . . . . . . . . $3-$8
**Movable ears:** . . . . . . . . . . . . $20-$25

*Droopy, with painted ears.* $3-$8

*Droopy, with movable ears.* **$20-$25**

### Duck (whistle)
No feet and with feet

**No feet:** . . . . . . . . . . . . . . . . . $45-$55
**With feet:** . . . . . . . . . . . . . . $30-$40

*Duck, whistle with feet.* **$30-$40**

### Duck with Flower

Early 1970s, no feet

Many head, flower, and beak color combinations can be found. Black, orange, and yellow are the hardest head colors to find and usually sell for twice as much as other color variations.

**Value:** . . . . . . . . . . . . . . . . . $80-$100
**Yellow head:** . . . . . . . . . . . . $125-$150
**Black or orange head:** . . . . . . . $175-$200

*Duck with Flower.* **$80-$100**

*Duck, versions with yellow head $125-$150, green head $80-$100, and orange head. $175-$200*

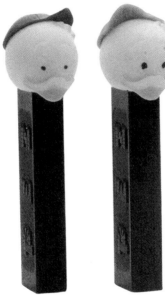

*Duck Nephews,
original version.*
**$30-$40**

## Duck Nephews

Originals are from the late 1970s, footed versions are from the late
1980s to 1990s. Variations can be found of this dispenser with large
and small pupils. The early version is also known as "Duck Child"
and was only produced with blue or green hats; the later versions
were produced with red hats, in addition to blue and green.

**Originals:** . . . . . . . . . . . . . . $30-$40
**With feet:** . . . . . . . . . . . . . . $5-$10

*Duck Nephews, with feet.* **$5-$10**

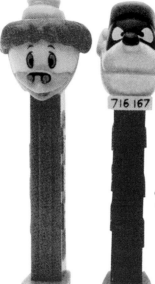

*Ducktails Gyro
Gearloose* **(L)** *$5-$8,
and Bouncer Beagle*
**(R)**. *$5-$8*

## Ducktails
Early 1990s, with feet

| | |
|---|---|
| **Gyro Gearloose:** . . . . . . . . . . . | $5-$8 |
| **Bouncer Beagle:** . . . . . . . . . . . | $5-$8 |
| **Webagail or Webby:** . . . . . . . . | $5-$8 |

*Ducktails Webagail or Webby.* **$5-$8**

## Dumbo
Late 1970s, no feet and with feet
**No feet: . . . . . . . . . . . . . . . . . $50-$60**
**With feet: . . . . . . . . . . . . . . . $30-$50**
**A very rare softhead version**
**also exists: . . . . . . . . . . . . . $3000+**

*Dumbo, no feet. $50-$60*

*Dumbo, with feet* **(L)** **$30-$50**, *and no feet.* **$50-$60**

*E.T.* **$2-$4**

**E.T.**
2002, with feet
**Value:** . . . . . . . . . . . . . . . . . . **$2-$4**

## Easter Bunny
1950s to current, no feet and with feet

| | |
|---|---|
| Bunny A, no feet, 1950s: | $200-$250 |
| Bunny B, no feet, 1950s: | $250-$300 |
| Fat Ear Bunny, no feet, 1960s-1970s: | $25-$40 |
| Fat Ear Bunny, with feet: | $10-$20 |
| Bunny D, 1990s: | $2-$4 |
| Bunny E, (current): | $1-$2 |

*Bunny B from the 1950s is a tough find.* **$250-$300**
*(From the Maryann Kennedy collection.)*

*Easter Bunny.* **(L to R)** *Bunny A* **$200-$250**, *Fat Ear Bunny, no feet* **$25-$40**, *Bunny D* **$2-$4**, *and Bunny E.* **$1-$2**

*Fat Ear bunnies, with feet* **(L)** *$10-$20, and no feet* **(R)**. *$25-$40*

*Fat Ear Bunny variations, no feet.* **$25-$40**

## Eerie Spectres (Also known as Softhead Monsters)

Late 1970s, no feet

This group is very popular among collectors. There are two variations for each character—"Made in Hong Kong" and "Hong Kong." These are the two different markings used on the back of the head with the "Hong Kong" mark being a bit harder to find. There is also a very distinct difference in face color between the two. The stems of these dispensers are always marked "Made in the USA." The six characters in the series are Air Spirit, Diabolic, Scarewolf, Spook, Vamp, and Zombie.

**"Made in Hong Kong":** . . . . . . $200-$250
**"Hong Kong":** . . . . . . . . . . . $225-$275

*"Made in Hong Kong" version of Air Spirit.*
**$200-$250**

*"Hong Kong" version of Air Spirit.* **$225-$275**

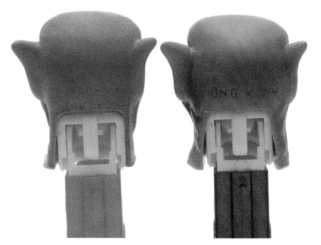

*Identifying marks on the back of the head.*

*"Made in Hong Kong" Zombie.* **$200-$250**

*"Hong Kong" Zombie.* **$225-$275**

*"Hong Kong" Vamp.* **$225-$250**

*"Made in Hong Kong" version of Vamp.* **$200-$250**

*"Made in Hong Kong" Diabolic.* **$200-$250**

*"Hong Kong" Diabolic.* **$225-$250**

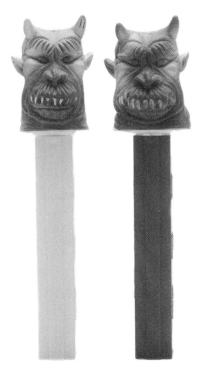

*"Made in Hong Kong" version* **(L)** *$200-$250, and "Hong Kong"*
*Spook* **(R)**. *$225-$275*

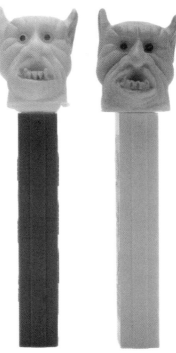

*"Made in Hong Kong" version* (**L**) **$200-$250**, *and "Hong Kong"*
*Scarewolf* (**R**) **$225-$275**.

*Hand-painted heads can vary greatly in detail.*

### Elephant (Also known as Circus Elephant or Big Top Elephant)

Early 1970s, no feet

There are three different variations to the elephant regarding its head gear—flat hat, pointy hat, and hair. The elephant came in many different color combinations, some of which, such as the pink head variation, are tough to find.

Flat hat:. . . . . . . . . . . . . . . . $100-$125
Pointy hat: . . . . . . . . . . . . . $125-$150
Hair: . . . . . . . . . . . . . . . . . $150-$175

*Elephant, with pointy hat.* **$125-$150**

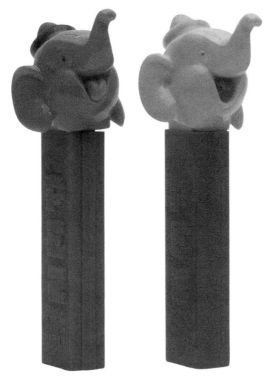

*More color variations for elephant with pointy hat.* **$125-$150**

*Elephant, with flat hat.* **$100-$125**
*(Pink elephant from the Maryann Kennedy collection.)*

*Elephant, with hair.* **$150-$175**

*Some variations of elephants with flat hats.* **$100-$125**
*(From the Johann Patek collection.)*

### Engineer
Mid-1970s, no feet
**Value:** . . . . . . . . . . . . . . . . . . **$175-$200**

*Engineer.* **$175-$200**

### Fireman
Early 1970s, no feet
The Fireman was available with a dark moustache. White moustache rarities must be sealed in the package to be considered a variation. Notice the light gray badge variation on the fireman on the far right.

**Darker badge:** ............ **$75-$90**
**Lighter badge:** ............ **$85-$100**

*Fireman with darker badge.* **$75-$90**

*Fireman with darker badge* **(L)** **$75-$90,**
*and lighter badge version* **(R)** **$85-$100**

## Fishman

Mid-1970s, no feet

The Fishman used the same mold as the Creature from the Black Lagoon, which was done as part of a Universal Studios Monsters series. The Creature was all green whereas the Fishman came with either a green or a black head and various colored stems.

**Value:** . . . . . . . . . . . . . . . . . **$175-$200**

*The all-green version of Fishman is known as the "Creature from the Black Lagoon."* **$175-$200**

*Various Fishman dispensers.* **$175-$200**

### Flintstones
Mid-1990s, with feet
Series includes Barney Rubble, Dino, Fred
Flintstone, and Pebbles Flintstone.
**Value:** . . . . . . . . . . . . . . . . . . **$1-$2**

*Fred Flintstone.* **$1-$2**

*Barney Rubble, Pebbles Flintstone, and Dino.* **$1-$2**

### Foghorn Leghorn

Early 1980s, no feet and with feet
Foghorn Leghorn can be found with either a
yellow or an orange beak.

**No feet:** . . . . . . . . . . . . . . . . $85-$100
**With feet:** . . . . . . . . . . . . . . $65-$85

*Foghorn Leghorn, with feet.* **$65-$85**

*Foghorn Leghorn, no feet.* $85-$100

*Football Player, with original vending box.*

## Football Player

Mid-1960s, no feet

This dispenser can be found in either red or blue and will either have a tape strip on the helmet (as shown) or a plastic strip that snaps on the front and back of the helmet. This version is very tough to find. The blank side of the stem with the triangle allowed kids to customize the dispenser with a pennant-shaped sticker of their favorite team.

**Tape-strip Helmet:** . . . . . . . . . $150-$175
**Snap-on Stripe:** . . . . . . . . . . . $250+

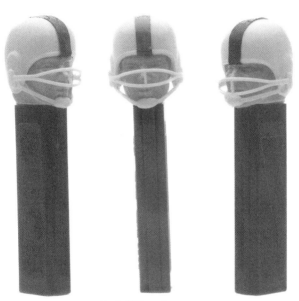

*Football Player dispensers.*

### Frog (whistle)
No feet and with feet

**No feet:** . . . . . . . . . . . . . . . . . $40-$50
**With feet:** . . . . . . . . . . . . . . . $30-$40

*Frog, whistle, no feet.* **$40-$50**

## Garfield

1990s, with feet

Two series featuring the comic strip character Garfield have been produced— the first in the early 1990s, the second in the late 1990s. The first series includes Garfield, Garfield with teeth, Garfield with visor, Arlene, and Nermal. The second series includes Garfield, Chef Garfield, Sleepy Garfield, Aviator Garfield, and Odie.

**First series: . . . . . . . . . . . . . . $2-$3 each**
**Second series: . . . . . . . . . . . $1-$2 each**

*A rare test mold version of Garfield.* **$NA**
*(From the Johann Patek collection.)*

*Garfield, first series Garfield, Garfield with teeth, and Garfield with visor.* **$2-$3**

*Garfield, first series Arlene and Nermal.* **$2-$3**

*Garfield, second series.* (**L to R**) *Garfield, Chef Garfield, Sleepy Garfield, Aviator Garfield, and Odie.* **$1-$2**

### Giraffe
Mid-1970s, no feet
This is one of the tougher animal dispensers
to find.
**Value:** .................. **$175-$200**

*Giraffe.* **$175-$200**

## Girl
Early 1970s, no feet and with feet
The Girl can be found with either blonde or
yellow hair.
**No feet:** . . . . . . . . . . . . . . . . . **$25-$35**
**With feet:** . . . . . . . . . . . . . . . **$5-$10**

*Girl, no feet.* $25-$35

*Another version of Girl, no feet.* **$25-$35**

*Vintage Golden Glows. The round base is the older of the two.* **$85-$125**
*(From the Johann Patek collection.)*

## Golden Glow

This dispenser was offered only as a mail-in premium and is tough
to find with finish in good condition—tarnish spots are common.
**Value:** . . . . . . . . . . . . . . . . . . **$85-$125**

*New Golden Glow 50th anniversary dispenser.* **$20**

*Newer Golden Glow regulars.* **$85-$125**
*(From the Johann Patek collection.)*

*Goofy, version D* (**L**) $2-$5, *and version E* (**R**). $1-$2

## Goofy

1970s to current, no feet and with feet

Several Goofy dispensers have been produced over the years.

Versions A, B, and C can be found with several face color variations.

**Goofy A, removable ears,**
**teeth, and nose, no feet:** . . . . . $30-$45
**Goofy B, removable ears**
**and teeth, no feet:** . . . . . . . . $25-$35
**Goofy C, removable**
**ears, no feet:** . . . . . . . . . . . . $25-$35
**Goofy C, with feet:** . . . . . . . . $15-$25
**Goofy D, late 1980s,**
**green hat, with feet:** . . . . . . . . $2-$5
**Goofy E, current:** . . . . . . . . . $1-$2

*Unusual variations of Goofy.* $NA
*(From the Johann Patek collection.)*

*Goofy, version B with several face variations.* **$25-$35**

*Goofy, version C with several face color variations.*
*Shown are both types, no feet* **$25-$35**, *and with feet.* **$15-$25**

*Two examples of the Gorilla.* **$80-$95**

## Gorilla
Mid-1970s, no feet
This dispenser was produced with a black, brown, or orange head.
**Value:** . . . . . . . . . . . . . . . . . . **$80-$95**

### Green Hornet
Late 1960s, no feet
The Green Hornet was produced in two
different versions—one with a small hat and
the other with a larger hat. The hat can be
found in either brown or gray.
**Version A (smaller hat):** . . . . . **$200-$225**
**Version B (larger hat):** . . . . . . **$175-$200**

*Green Hornet, version A with smaller hat.* **$200-$225**

*Close-up of the Green Hornet head.*

*Green Hornet, version B with larger hat.* **$175-$200**

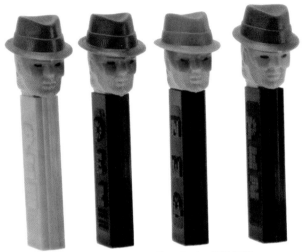

*Green Hornet variations with smaller hat.* **$200-$225**

*The very rare Groom dispenser.* **$500-$700**

## Groom

Late 1970s, no feet

A rare dispenser from the October 6, 1978, wedding of Robert and Claudia (relatives of a PEZ® executive).

**Value:** . . . . . . . . . . . . . . . . . . **$500-$700**

## Halloween Crystal Series
1999, with feet
This series was only available through a
PEZ® mail-in offer. The series includes a
Jack-o-Lantern and three different ghosts.
**Value: .................. $3-$5 each**

*Halloween Crystal series Jack-o-Lantern.* **$3-$5**

*Halloween Crystal series ghosts.* **$3-$5**

## Halloween Ghosts
Late 1990s, with feet
This non-glowing series was available in the U.S. for only a couple of years. Characters include: Naughty Neil, Slimy Sid, and Polly Pumpkin. These do not glow in the dark.
**Value:** . . . . . . . . . . . . . . . . . . **$1-$2 each**

*Halloween ghost.* **$1-$2**

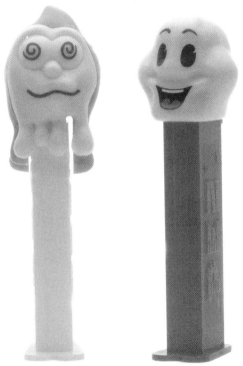

*Two additional Halloween ghosts.* **$1-$2**

### Halloween Glowing Ghosts

Late 1990s, with feet

This glowing version first sold only in Europe, not released in the U.S. assortment until 2002. Characters include: Happy Henry, Naughty Neil, Slimy Sid, and Polly Pumpkin.

**Value:** . . . . . . . . . . . . . . . . . **$1-$2 each**

*Halloween Glowing Ghost Happy Henry.* **$1-$2**

*Halloween Glowing Ghosts Naughty Neil, Slimy Sid, and Polly Pumpkin.* **$1-$2**

*Halloween Glowing Ghost Happy Henry glowing in the dark.*

*Halloween Glowing Ghost Polly Pumpkin glowing in the dark.*

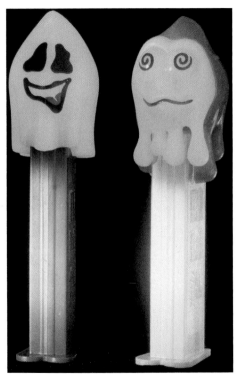

*Additional Halloween Glowing Ghosts with the lights out.*

## Henry Hawk
Early 1980s, no feet and with feet
**No feet:** . . . . . . . . . . . . . . . . . **$80-$100**
**With feet:** . . . . . . . . . . . . . . **$60-$75**

*Henry Hawk, with feet.* **$60-$75**

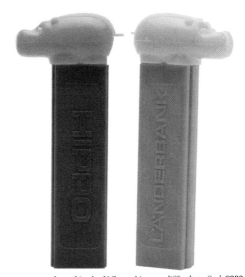

*The Hippo was not released in the U.S., and is very difficult to find.* **$900-$1000**

## Hippo

Early 1970s, no feet

Among the rarest of the animal dispensers, the hippo was not released in the United States and is very difficult to find. The Hippo is unusual in that it has an entire body on top of the stem, rather than just a head.

**Value:** . . . . . . . . . . . . . . . . . . **$900-$1000**

## Holiday 2002
**With feet:**. . . . . . . . . . . . . . . . $1-$2

*Holiday 2002 Reindeer.* **$1-$2**

*Holiday 2002 Santa, Snowman, Winter Bear, and Elf.* **$1-$2**

*Holiday Crystal Series Santa and Snowman.* **$3-$5**

## Holiday Crystal Series
1999, with feet
This series was only available through a PEZ® mail-in offer. The series includes Santa, Snowman, Witch, and Skull.
**Value: . . . . . . . . . . . . . . . . . $3-$5 each**

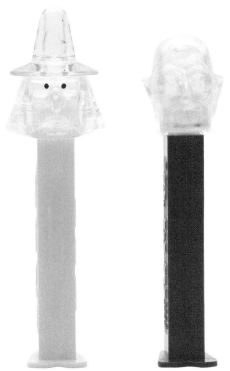

*Holiday Crystal Series Witch and Skull.* **$3-$5**

### Icee Bear
1990s, with feet
The earlier version of Icee Bear was not
issued in the U.S. The version made its
debut in the 1999 Christmas assortment. It
was revised in 2002.
**Early version, left and center:  . $5-$10 each**
**Far right: . . . . . . . . . . . . . . . . $1-$3**
**Current: . . . . . . . . . . . . . . . . $1-$2**

*1999 Christmas assortment Icee Bear.* **$1-$3**

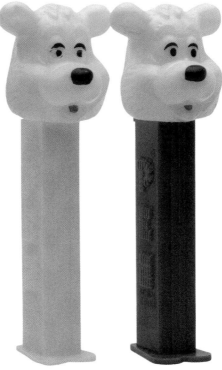

*Icee Bear, early version.* $5-$10

## Incredible Hulk

Late 1970s, no feet and with feet
The Incredible Hulk dispenser has been
produced in varying shades of green.

**Dark green, no feet:** . . . . . . . . $40-$50
**Light green, no feet:** . . . . . . . . $45-$55
**Light green, with feet:** . . . . . . $3-$5
**With teeth (current version,**
**released 1999):** . . . . . . . . . . . $1-$2

*1999 version of the Incredible Hulk, light green*
*with feet.* **$3-$5**

*Rare white eye version of the Incredible Hulk, dark green no feet.* **$NA**
*(From the Johann Patek collection.)*

*Incredible Hulk,* **(L to R)** *dark green* **$40-$50**, *light green no feet* **$45-$55**, *and light green with feet.* **$3-$5**

*Indian, whistle.* $25-$35

## Indian (whistle)
With feet
**Value:** . . . . . . . . . . . . . . . . . . $25-$35

*Indian Brave.* **$150-$175**

## Indian Brave
Early 1970s, no feet
**Value:** . . . . . . . . . . . . . . . . . . **$150-$175**

### Indian Chief
Early 1970s, no feet
The swirled headdress combinations are virtually endless. It is rumored the plastic used to make the headdress was molded from the ground up and re-melted remains of unsold Make-a-Face dispensers.

**Value:** .................. **$125-$150**
**White headdress:** .......... **$100-$125**

*Indian Chief.* **$125-$150**

*Indian Maiden.* **$125-$150**

# Indian Maiden
Mid-1970s, no feet
**Value:** . . . . . . . . . . . . . . . . . **$125-$150**

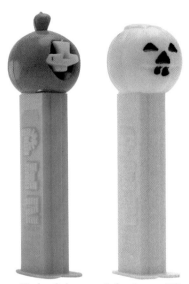

*Hard-to-find two-tone Jack-o-Lantern.* **$NA**
*(From the Johann Patek collection.)*

## Jack-o-Lantern
1980s, no feet and with feet

**Version A, die-cut**
**face, no feet:** .............. $20-$25
**Version A, with feet:** ........ $10-$15
**Version B:** ................ $2-$3
**Version C:** ................ $1-$2
**Version D glows**
**in the dark (current):** ........ $1-$2

*Jack-o-Lantern,* **(L to R)** *version A no feet* **$20-$25***, version A with feet* **$10-$15***, version B* **$2-$3***, and version C.* **$1-$2**

*Variation of the multi-piece-faced Jerry.* **$10-$15**

## Jerry

Early 1980s to current, no feet and with feet

One half of MGM's famous cat and mouse duo. Not released in the U.S. There are many variations of this dispenser.

No feet: . . . . . . . . . . . . . . . . $30-$40
Thin Feet: . . . . . . . . . . . . . . $5-$10
Multi-piece face: . . . . . . . . . $10-$15
With feet: . . . . . . . . . . . . . . $4-$8
Current: . . . . . . . . . . . . . . . $2-$3

*Another variation of the multi-piece-faced Jerry.* **$10-$15**

*Jerry,* **(L to R)** *no feet* **$30-$40***, thin feet* **$5-$10***, and multi-piece face.* **$10-$15**

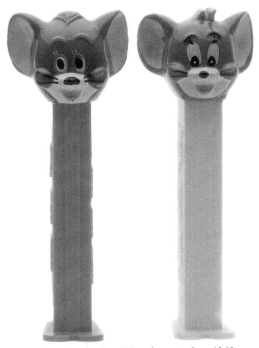

*Jerry, with feet* **(L)** *$4-$8, and current release. $2-$3*

*Rare ear insert versions of Jerry and Tuffy.* **$NA**
*(From the Johann Patek collection.)*

## Jiminy Cricket

Early 1970s, no feet
With many small pieces making up his costume,
Jiminy Cricket is a tough dispenser to find
complete.

**Value: . . . . . . . . . . . . . . . . . $200-$250**

*Jiminy Cricket.* **$200-$250**

*Another angle of the Jiminy Cricket dispenser.*

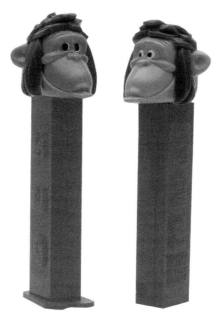

*King Louie,* **(L to R)** *no feet* $30-$45, *and with feet.* $25-$35

## King Louie
Late 1960s, no feet and with feet

No feet: . . . . . . . . . . . . . . . . . $30-$45
With feet: . . . . . . . . . . . . . . . $25-$35
Rare and unusual
color variations: . . . . . . . . . . . $300+

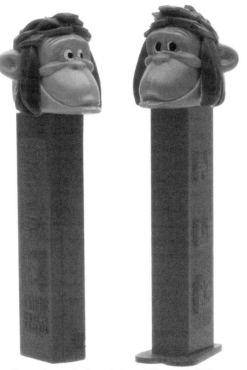

*Rare and unusual color variations of King Louie.* **$300+**

## Knight

Early 1970s, no feet
The Knight was available in three colors—
red, black, or white. The white knight is
the hardest to find. The plume color on
the helmet must always match the stem in
order to be correct.

**Red:** ................... $300-$350
**Black:** .................. $350-$375
**White:** .................. $500-$600

*Knight with red stem.* **$300-$350**

*Knight with white stem.* **$500-$600** *Knight with black stem.* **$350-$375**

### Koala (whistle)
No feet and with feet

**No feet:** . . . . . . . . . . . . . . . . . $35-$45
**With feet:** . . . . . . . . . . . . . . . $15-$25

*Koala whistle with feet.* **$15-$25**

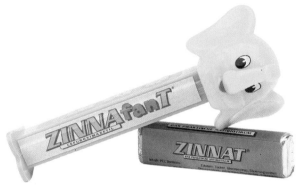

*"Zinnafant" elephant. Done by a European drug company to promote a new antibiotic drug called "Zinnat." Should come with matching candy pack to be considered complete.* **$25-$35**

## Kooky Zoo Series

Late 1990s, with feet

Series includes Blinky Bill, a koala and licensed Australian comic character, Lion, Gator, Hippo, and Elephant. A crystal series was available in 1999 through a PEZ® mail-in offer.

A pink elephant and a lion were also released by PEZ® Candy Inc. as part of their "misfits" mail-in offer.

| | |
|---|---|
| **Value:** | **$2-$6 each** |
| **Crystal series:** | **$3-$5 each** |
| **Misfit Elephant and Lion:** | **$3-$5 each** |
| **Zinnafant Elephant:** | **$25-$30** |

*Kooky Zoo series characters* **(L to R)** *Blinky Bill,
Lion, Gator, Hippo, and Elephant.* **$2-$6**

## Lamb
1970s, no feet and with feet

**No feet:** . . . . . . . . . . . . . . . . . **$20-$30**
**With feet:** . . . . . . . . . . . . . . . **$1-$3**

*Lamb, no feet.* **$20-$30**

*Lamb,* **(L to R)** *no feet* **$20-$30***, with feet.* **$1-$3**

*Lamb, whistle with feet.* **$15-$25**

## Lamb (whistle)
No feet and with feet
**No feet:** . . . . . . . . . . . . . . . . $25-$35
**With feet:** . . . . . . . . . . . . . . $15-$25

### Lil Bad Wolf
Mid-1960s, no feet and with feet

**No feet:** . . . . . . . . . . . . . . . . . . $30-$50
**With feet:** . . . . . . . . . . . . . . . $20-$35

*Lil Bad Wolf, no feet.* **$30-$50**

**Lil Lion**
Late 1960s, no feet
**Value:** . . . . . . . . . . . . . . . . . $70-$90

*Lil Lion.* **$70-$90**

## Lion with Crown

Mid-1970s, no feet

This dispenser can be found with several subtle green face color variations and many other different color combinations. The very tough to find red face with white crown goes for twice the price of other variations. Some rare variations can sell for more than double the price.

**Value:** .................. **$125-$175**
**Red face/white crown:** ...... **$200-$250**

*Hard-to-find Lion with Crown variation.* **$200-$250**
*(From the Johann Patek collection.)*

*Variations of the Lion with Crown.* **$125-$175**
*(From the Maryann Kennedy collection.)*

## Lions Club

1962, no feet

A unique, interesting, and hard-to-find dispenser. Consul Haas was the president of Lions Club, Austria. He commissioned the dispenser for the purpose of handing them out to members who attended the 1962 International Lions Club convention in Nice, France. After the convention, the few pieces of remaining stock had the inscribed stem removed and replaced with a generic PEZ® stem. It was sold in the Circus assortment.

**Inscribed stem:** . . . . . . . . . . **$3000+**
**Generic stem:** . . . . . . . . . . . **$2000+**

*A red head variation of the Lions Club dispenser with generic stem.* **$2000+**

*Lions Club dispenser with inscribed stem.* **$3000+**

*Close-up of stem inscription.*

*Magic PEZ® dispenser.* **$3-$6**

## Magic PEZ® dispenser

Dispenses candy from the hat and has an additional compartment
on the bottom that holds an extra pack of candy that you can make
disappear then magically re-appear! Can be found in many different
color combinations.

**Value:** . . . . . . . . . . . . . . . . . **$3-$6 each**

### Maharajah

Early 1970s, no feet

There are several variations to this dispenser. One version, made in Hong Kong, has a slightly different turban than the others.

**"Hong Kong" version:** ....... $75-$85
**Darker green turban:** ....... $80-$100
**Lighter green turban:** ....... $60-$80

*A rare black variation.* **$NA**
*(From the Johann Patek collection.)*

*Maharajah, from the early 1970s. Notice the one on the far left. His turban is shaped slightly different than the other two. This is the "Hong Kong" version $75-$85; the one in the middle has a darker green turban $80-$100, and the lighter green one on the right is the most common of the three. $60-$80*

*A loose Make-a-Face dispenser.* **$2500-$3000**

## Make-a-Face

Early 1970s, no feet
This dispenser first appeared in 1972,
but was quickly discontinued as it
had too many tiny pieces that could
be easily removed and swallowed by a
child. Also, the dispenser was poorly
packaged—the bubble frequently
came loose from the card spilling the
parts, and rendering it unsaleable. It is
rumored what stock was left of these
after they were discontinued was ground
up, re-melted, and used to mold the
headdress for the Indian Chief. The U.S.
version contained 17 separate pieces
and the European 16, not counting the
shoes. This is a very difficult dispenser
to find still intact on the card.

**U.S. version m.o.c.:** . . . . . . . . **$3000+**
**European version m.o.c.:** . . . . **$2500+**

*A trio of Make-a-Faces.* **$2500-$3000**
*(From the Johann Patek collection.)*

*Front of U.S. card.*
*(From the Johann Patek collection.)*

*Back of U.S. card.*
*(From the Johann Patek collection.)*

*Front of European card.*
*(From the Johann Patek collection.)*

*Back of European card.*
*(From the Johann Patek collection.)*

## Mary Poppins

Early 1970s, no feet
This dispenser is very difficult to find. As pictured, an even harder to find "painted cheek" variation. One rumor has it this dispenser was in early production when Disney didn't approve the likeness causing PEZ® to halt further distribution, making this a true rarity!

**Value:** . . . . . . . . . . . . . . . . . . **$850-$1000**
**Painted cheeks:** . . . . . . . . . . . **$950-$1100**

*Mary Poppins, with painted cheeks.* **$950-$1100**

*Merlin Mouse,* **(L)** *no feet* **$20-$30***, with feet.* **$12-$15**

## Merlin Mouse
Early 1980s, no feet and with feet
**No feet:** . . . . . . . . . . . . . . . . . $20-$30
**With feet:** . . . . . . . . . . . . . . $12-$15

## Mexican
Mid-1960s, no feet
With removable hat, goatee, and earrings, this
one can be tough to find with all of his pieces.
**Value:** . . . . . . . . . . . . . . . . . **$200-$250**

*Mexican.* **$200-$250**

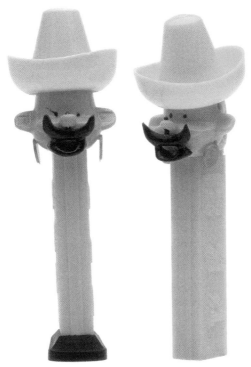

*Additional views of Mexican.*

## Mickey Mouse

Early 1960s-Present, no feet and with feet
Mickey Mouse has been one of the most
popular PEZ® dispensers over the years
and has gone through many variations.

**Die-cut stem with
painted face, early 1960s:** . . . . $300-$400
**Die-cut face, early
1960s, no feet:** . . . . . . . . . . $100-$140
**Version A, removable
nose, early 1970s, no feet:** . . . $20-$30
**Version B, molded
nose, early 1980s, no feet:** . . . $15-$25
**Version B, with feet:** . . . . . . . . $10-$15
**Version C, stencil eyes, 1990s:** $2-$3
**Mickey and Minnie Mouse,
current release:** . . . . . . . . . . . $1-$2
**Softhead version (rare):** . . . . . $3000+

*Rare test mold of Mickey Mouse.* $NA
*(From the Johann Patek collection.)*

*Mickey Mouse with die-cut face pictured* **(L)** **$100-$140**, *rare painted version* **(R)**. *$NA*

*Mickey Mouse with die-cut stem and painted face.* **$300-$400**
*Rare variations of the painted-face Mickey.* **$NA**
*(From the Johann Patek collection.)*

*Rare variations of the painted-face Mickey.* **$NA**
*(From the Johann Patek collection.)*

*Mickey and Minnie Mouse, late 1990s edition.* **$1-$2**

*Version B Mickey Mouse no feet* **(L)** **$15-$25**, *version C* **(R).** **$2-$3**

### Mimic the Monkey (Also known as Monkey with Ball Cap)

Mid-1970s, no feet and with feet
Many different head colors were produced, making this an especially fun dispenser to try and collect all variations. Head colors include orange, yellow, red, and blue.

No feet: . . . . . . . . . . . . . . . . . $45-$60
With feet: . . . . . . . . . . . . . . . $40-$50

*Mimic the Monkey is also known as "Monkey with Ball Cap," no feet.* **$45-$60**

*Another color variation of Mimic the Monkey no feet.* **$45-$60**

## Monkey (whistle)
No feet and with feet

**No feet:** . . . . . . . . . . . . . . . . . $30-$40
**With feet:** . . . . . . . . . . . . . . $25-$30

*Monkey, whistle with feet.* **$25-$30**

*Monkey Sailor.* **$60-$80**

## Monkey Sailor

Late 1960s, no feet
The same dispenser was used as Donkey
Kong Jr. with one exception, a small
transparent sticker was added on his cap
with the letter "J." The Donkey Kong
Jr. was a 1984 Ralston Purina cereal
premium.

**Monkey Sailor:** . . . . . . . . . . . **$60-$80**
**Donkey Kong Jr. with box:** . . . . **$400-$500**

*Side view of Monkey Sailor.*

## Mowgli
Late 1960s, no feet and with feet

**No feet:** . . . . . . . . . . . . . . . . . **$30-$40**
**With feet:** . . . . . . . . . . . . . . **$25-$35**

*Mowgli, no feet.* **$30-$40**

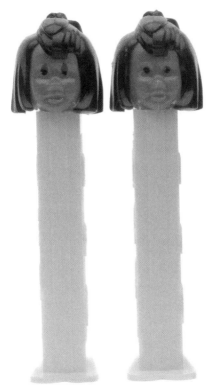

*Mowgli, with feet.* **$25-$35**

### Mr. Mystic

No feet

Some doubt the authenticity of this piece, citing it as nothing more than the head of Zorro with a ringmaster hat on it. Currently there is documentation from PEZ® International that states his existence.

**Value:** . . . . . . . . . . . . . . . . . **$500+**

*Mr. Mystic.* **$500+**
*(From the Maryann Kennedy collection.)*

## Mr. Ugly

Early 1970s, no feet and with feet
This really is a homely guy! Several
variations to the face coloring exist and
differ in value.

**Chartreuse green face:** . . . . . . $75-$95
**Aqua green face:** . . . . . . . . . . $80-$90
**Olive green face:** . . . . . . . . . . $60-$75
**With feet:** . . . . . . . . . . . . . . . $45-$65

*Mr. Ugly with chartreuse green face.* $75-$95

*Mr. Ugly with aqua-green faces* (**L & C**)
**$80-$90**, *and olive green face* (**R**). **$60-$75**

## Muppets

Early 1990s, with feet
Included in the series are Fozzie Bear, Gonzo,
Kermit the Frog, and Miss Piggy. A harder
to find version with eyelashes exists of Miss
Piggy.

**Miss Piggy with eyelashes: . . . $10-$15**
**Miss Piggy (common**
**and current versions): . . . . . . . $1-$3**
**Fozzie, Gonzo, and Kermit: . . . $1-$2**

*Current version of Kermit the Frog.* **$1-$2**

*Rare Gonzo test mold variation.* **$NA**

*Miss Piggy* (**L to R**) *with eyelashes* **$10-$15**, *common version* **$1-$3**, *and current version.* **$1-$3**

*Kermit, Fozzie Bear, and Gonzo.* **$1-$2**

## Nintendo

Late 1990s, with feet

A series not available in the U.S. featuring characters from Nintendo's video games. Dispensers include Diddy Kong, Yoshi, Koopa Trooper, and Mario.

**Value:** .................. **$2-$3 each**

*Mario.* $2-$3

(L to R) *Diddy Kong, Yoshi, and Koopa Trooper.* $2-$3

## Octopus

Early 1970s, no feet
The Octopus can be found in red, orange, or black.

**Orange:** . . . . . . . . . . . . . . . . . $85-$95
**Black:** . . . . . . . . . . . . . . . . . . $90-$120
**Red:** . . . . . . . . . . . . . . . . . . . $125-$150

*Octopus.* **$85-$95**

*Another Octopus variation.* **$85-$95**

### Olympic Snowman
No feet
This dispenser was made for the 1976
winter Olympics in Innsbruck, Austria. A
very hard-to-find dispenser, it can also be
found in a "short nose" version.
**Value: . . . . . . . . . . . . . . . . . . $500-$600**

*Long-nose version of the Olympic Snowman.*
**$500-$600**

*Olympic Snowman still on card.*
*(From the Johann Patek collection.)*

## Olympic Wolves (also called Vucko (voo sh-co) wolves)

With feet

This hard-to-find dispenser was made for the 1984 Olympic games in Sarajevo, Yugoslavia. Variations exist without hat, with hat, and with bobsled helmet.

Wolf, no hat: . . . . . . . . . . . . $350-$450
Wolf, no hat,
unusual brown nose: . . . . . . . $375-$425
Wolf with hat: . . . . . . . . . . . $450-$550
Wolf with bobsled helmet: . . . . $500-$600

*Vucko with bobsled helmet.* **$500-$600**
*(From the Maryann Kennedy collection.)*

*Vucko shown here with a paper insert.*
*(From the Maryann Kennedy collection.)*

*Notice the Olympic rings and Olympic symbol molded into the head.*
*(From the Maryann Kennedy collection.)*

*Vucko, without hat.* $350-$450
*(From the Maryann Kennedy collection.)*

*Vucko, with hat* **(L & C)** *$450-$550, with red bobsled helmet* **(R)**. *$500-$600*

### One-Eyed Monster
Early 1970s, no feet and with feet
This dispenser was available with either
an orange, brown, black, gray, pink, or
yellow head.
No feet: . . . . . . . . . . . . . . . . . $80-$100
With feet: . . . . . . . . . . . . . . . $65-$80

*One-eyed Monster, no feet.* **$80-$100**

## Owl (whistle)
With feet
The Owl is very rare and only a few are
known to exist.
**Value: . . . . . . . . . . . . . . . . . $2000+**

*Very rare Owl whistle.* **$2000+**
*(From the Maryann Kennedy collection.)*

*Two rare variations of the Panda—the yellow and red heads.* **$300+**
*(From the Maryann Kennedy collection.)*

## Panda

Early 1970s, no feet and with feet

The Panda has undergone a few modest changes but can still be found today. Rare and hard-to-find colors include the yellow and red head versions.

**Removable eyes
version (oldest):** . . . . . . . . . . . $25-$35
**Yellow or red head
(with removable eyes):** . . . . . . $300+
**No feet, stencil eyes:** . . . . . . . $10-$20
**Current version:** . . . . . . . . . . $1-$2

*Panda,* **(L to R)** *current version* **$1-$2,** *stencil eyes* **$10-$20,**
*and removable eyes.* **$25-$35**

*(L to R) Panda whistle with stencil eyes* **$5-$10**, *and removable eyes.* **$20-$25**

## Panda (whistle)

No feet and with feet

The Panda was made with removable eyes and with stencil eyes.

**Removable eyes, no feet:** .... $25-$35
**Removable eyes, with feet:** ... $20-$25
**Stencil eyes, with feet:** ...... $5-$10

**Panther**
Late 1970s, no feet
**Value:** .................. $75-$100

*Unusual Panther variation.* **$NA**
*(From the Johann Patek collection.)*

## Parrot (whistle)

No feet and with feet
A rare variation of the Parrot exists
with a yellow head and a red beak;
more common versions have a red head
with a yellow beak.

**No feet:** . . . . . . . . . . . . . . . . . **$15-$20**
**With feet:** . . . . . . . . . . . . . . **$5-$10**
**Yellow head, red beak:** . . . . . . **$300+**

*Parrot whistle with rare yellow head and red beak.* **$300+**
*(From the Maryann Kennedy collection.)*

*Peppermint Patty,* **$1-$2**, *and Joe Cool.* **$1-$3**

## Peanuts

Early 1990s to current, with feet
Characters include Charlie Brown, Lucy,
Snoopy, Woodstock, and Peppermint Patty.
Several variations exist for each.

Charlie Brown, smiling:  ..... $1-$2
Charlie Brown,
frowning (non-U.S.): ........ $5-$10
Charlie Brown, tongue
showing (non-U.S.): ........ $5-$10
Charlie Brown, eyes
closed (non-U.S.):  ........ $50-$60
Lucy, common version: ...... $1-$2
Lucy, white around eyes: ..... $50-$75
Lucy, white face
(known as "Psycho Lucy"): ... $75-$90
Peppermint Patty: .......... $1-$2
Snoopy:  ................ $1-$3
Snoopy as "Joe Cool":....... $1-$3
Woodstock, common version:  . $1-$2
Woodstock with feathers
(black markings on the
top and back of his head): .... $3-$5

*Charlie Brown,* **(L to R)** *smiling* **$1-$2**, *frowning* **$5-$10**, *and with tongue showing.* **$5-$10**

*Lucy,* **(L to R)** *common version* **$1-$2**, *white around eyes* **$50-$75**, *and white face ( Psycho Lucy).* **$75-$90**

*Woodstock, common version* (**L**) **$1-$2**, *Woodstock with feathers* (**C**) **$3-$5**, *and Snoopy.* **$1-$3**

*Peanuts 2000. Charlie Brown* **$1-$2***, Lucy* **$1-$2***, Snoopy* **$1-$3***,
and Woodstock.* **$1-$2**

**Penguin (whistle)**
With feet
**Value:** . . . . . . . . . . . . . . . . . . $5-$10

*Penguin, whistle.* $5-$10

**Peter Pan**
Late 1960s, no feet
**Value:** . . . . . . . . . . . . . . . . . . $175-$225

*Peter Pan.* **$175-$225**

## Peter PEZ®

Late 1970s, no feet and with feet
A dispenser featuring the clown mascot of
the PEZ® Candy company. The original
was produced in the late 1970s and a
remake came out in the early 1990s.

**Original version, no feet:** .... $50-$75
**Remake (1993 to 2001):** ..... $2-$4
**Current:** ................. $1-$2
**"Rico" variation:** .......... $20-$30

*Peter PEZ® "Rico" variation. "Rico" means
candy.* **$20-$30**

*2001 version of Peter PEZ®, (L) mail-order variation dispenser glows in the dark.* **$2-$4**

### Petunia Pig
Early 1980s, no feet and with feet

**No feet:** . . . . . . . . . . . . . . . . . $40-$50
**With feet:** . . . . . . . . . . . . . . . $30-$40

*Petunia Pig, with feet.* **$30-$40**

### PIF the Dog

With feet
PIF was offered as a premium in a German "YPS" comic in 1989. If you look closely you can see his name PIF on his left ear.

**Value:** . . . . . . . . . . . . . . . . . . **$85-$100**

*PIF the Dog.* **$85-$100**

### Pig (whistle)
No feet and with feet

**No feet:** . . . . . . . . . . . . . . . . . . $50-$60
**With feet:** . . . . . . . . . . . . . . . . $35-$45

*Pig, with feet.* $35-$45

## Pilgrim

Mid-1970s, no feet
The Pilgrim can be found with either a white or yellow hatband.

**Value:** .................. **$125-$150**

*Pilgrim.* **$125-$150**

*Pilot.* **$75-$200**

*Stewardess.* **$75-$200**

## Pilot and Stewardess
Mid-1970s, no feet

| | |
|---|---|
| **Pilot:** . . . . . . . . . . . . . . . . . . . | **$175-$200** |
| **Stewardess:** . . . . . . . . . . . . . | **$175-$200** |

### Pink Panther

Late 1990s, with feet
Not available in the U.S., this series
featured the Pink Panther, Inspector
Clousseau, Ant, and Aardvark.

Value: . . . . . . . . . . . . . . . . . . $2-$3 each
2002 remake: . . . . . . . . . . . . $2-$5

*2002 version of the Pink Panther.* **$2-$5**

*1990s Pink Panther series (**L to R**) Pink Panther, Inspector Clouseau, Ant, and Aardvark.* **$2-$3**

### Pinocchio
Early 1960s, no feet
Two versions of Pinocchio were made—
one in the early 1960s and the other in the
early 1970s. The earlier version (A) can be
found with either a red or yellow hat.
**Version A: . . . . . . . . . . . . . . . $175-$225**
**Version B: . . . . . . . . . . . . . . . $140-$165**

*Pinocchio, A version.* **$175-$225**

## Pirate
Early 1970s, no feet
Variations can be found in the Pirate's
bandana and in his skin tone.
**Value:** ................... **$60-$85**

*Pirate.* **$60-$85**

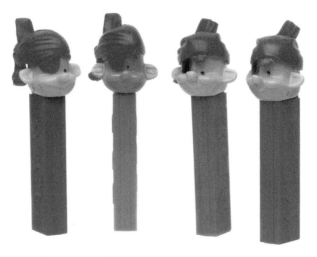

*More Pirate variations. The unusual orange-flesh variation is pictured second from left.* **$60-$85**

*Easter Playworld set.* **$20-$25**

## Playworld Sets

Early 1990s, with feet, Non-U.S.

These sets featured a single dispenser along with a matching body part. The sets usually have a theme such as Easter or Christmas. After opening the package, the cardboard piece inserted with it would unfold into three sections. It contained related scenery which could serve as a backdrop in which to play with the dispenser.

Easter set: . . . . . . . . . . . . . . . $20-$25
Christmas set: . . . . . . . . . . . $10-$15
Shell Gas set: . . . . . . . . . . . $20-$25

*Christmas Playworld set.* **$10-$15**

*Shell Gas Playworld set.* **$20-$25**

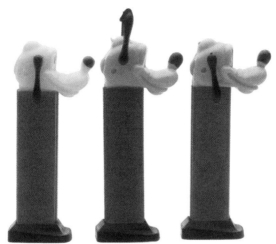

*Pluto, first appeared in the early 1960s.* **(L to R)** *Original "Hong Kong" version* **$20-$25**, *original version* **$25-$30**, *and caramel variation of original version.*
**$25-$30**

## Pluto
Early 1960s to current, no feet and with feet
Several versions of Pluto, Mickey Mouse's faithful dog, have been produced through the years.

**Version A, round head**
**and movable ears, no feet:** ... $25-$30
**Version A, "Hong Kong":** .... $20-$25
**Version B, flat head**
**and movable ears:** ......... $10-$15
**Version C, molded ears:** ..... $2-$5
**Version D, (current):** ........ $1-$2

*Pluto, the two on the left are version B and are sometimes called the flathead version* **$10-$15**, *version C is second from right* **$2-$5**, *and the far right is version D.* **$1-$2**

**Pokémon**
2001, with feet
**Value:** . . . . . . . . . . . . . . . . . . $1-$4

*Pikachu.* $1-$4

**(L to R)** *Meowth, Mew, Psyduck, and Koffing.* **$1-$4**

## Policeman
Early 1970s, no feet
**Value:** . . . . . . . . . . . . . . . . . . **$50-$75**

*Policeman.* **$50-$75**

*Additional Policeman variations.* **$50-$75**

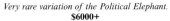

*Very rare variation of the Political Elephant.*
**$6000+**

*(From the Johann Patek collection.)*

## Political Elephant

No feet

This is an extremely rare dispenser, only a few are known to exist. It is thought to represent the elephant of the Republican political party. In early 1997 an old file was discovered in the PEZ® factory in Connecticut containing a press release and an old photo of a special set of dispensers. The press release was dated June 13, 1961 and had the heading "President Kennedy receives PEZ® souvenirs on his visit to Vienna." It went on to detail the set and then said "To the President of the United States of America J.F. Kennedy with the Compliments of PEZ®." The set contained in a wooden, cigar-like box had three dispensers; a Donkey for the President (to represent the Democratic Party), a Golden Glow for Jackie, a Bozo die-cut for Caroline, and three packs of candy for each. To date, the Donkey of this set has yet to surface. The elephant as pictured has a shiny, golden-colored head with his trunk extending over the top of his head.

**Value:** . . . . . . . . . . . . . . . . . **$6000+**

*Another rare variation of the Political Elephant.* **$6000+**
*(From the Johann Patek collection.)*

## Pony (also known as Pony-Go-Round)

Early 1970s, no feet

This dispenser can be found in MANY different colors and it's fun to search for variations. Some are very difficult to find such as the green, pink, and purple heads and these versions can bring up to five times as much as the more common color combinations.

**Value (common color combinations):** . . . . . . . . . . . . $100-$150

*Pony.* **$100-$150**

*(From the Maryann Kennedy collection.)*

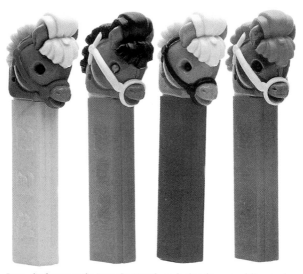

*Pony, also known as the Pony-Go-Round, can be found in many different colors.
The green, pink, and purple heads are less common variations and can bring up
to five times as much as more common color variations.*
*(From the Maryann Kennedy collection.)*

## Popeye

Late 1950s to late 1970s, no feet

Some believe Popeye was the first licensed character PEZ® ever used on a dispenser. Brutus and Olive Oyl were produced in the mid-1960s and usually are found with missing or chipped paint on their faces.

**Popeye, original version, hat is molded to the head:** .............. $150-$175

**Popeye B, plain face:** ....... $125-$150

**Popeye C, with pipe (note the pipe is the same piece used on**

**Mickey Mouse's nose):** ...... $100-$125

**Brutus:** ................. $250-$275

**Olive Oyl:** .............. $275-$325

*Olive Oyl.* **$275-$325**

*Brutus.* $250-$275

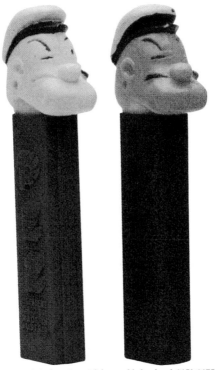

*Popeye, original version with hat molded to head.* **$150-$175**

*Popeye, version B* (**L**) **$125-$150**, *version B with removable pipe*
(**C & R**). **$100-$125**

*Practical Pig, version A with feet* **(L)** **$25-$35**, *and no feet* **(R)**. **$35-$50**

## Practical Pig

1960s, no feet and with feet

Two versions were produced—the earlier version (version A) has a flat hat and the later version (B) produced in the 1970s, has a wavy hat.

**Version A, no feet:** . . . . . . . . $35-$50
**Version A, with feet:** . . . . . . . . $25-$35
**Version B, no feet:** . . . . . . . . $40-$60
**Version B, with feet:** . . . . . . . . $30-$40

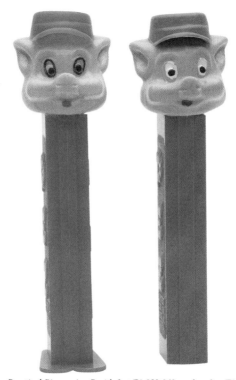

*Practical Pig, version B with feet* **(L)** **$30-$40**, *and no feet* **(R)**.

### Psychedelic Flower
Late 1960s, no feet
Very much a product of their time, these dispensers came packaged with flower flavor candy. They can be found with several different stickers including, "mod pez," "go-go pez," and different "luv pez" versions on at least one side. The side that has the sticker will be completely smooth. Some dispensers had stickers on both sides and are considered to be worth a bit more than a one-sticker dispenser.

*Original Psychedelic Flower.* **$450-$550**

*Hard–to–find yellow and deep red flower variations.* **$NA**

A collector's edition remake was produced in the late 1990s and was available from PEZ® through a mail-in offer. The remake versions have the raised PEZ® logo on the stem and do not have stickers on either side. They are also marked with a copyright symbol and 1967—the originals do not have a date on them.

**Original:** . . . . . . . . . . . . . . . . $450-$550
**Remake, m.o.c.:** . . . . . . . . . $15-$20

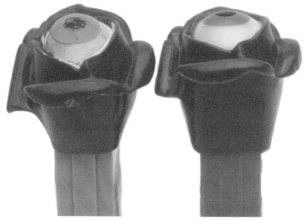

*Comparison of a vintage Psychedelic Flower* **(L)** *and a remake.*

## Psychedelic Hand
Late 1960s, no feet
The Hand also came packaged with
flower flavor candy, and will have at
least one sticker. The side that has the
sticker will be completely smooth. Some
dispensers had stickers on both sides and
are considered to be worth a bit more
than a one-sticker dispenser.
A collector's edition remake was produced
in the late 1990s and was only available
through a PEZ® mail-in offer. The
remake versions have the raised PEZ®
logo on the stem and do not have stickers
on either side. They are also marked
with a copyright symbol and 1967—the
originals do not have a date on them.

**Original:** . . . . . . . . . . . . . . . . . $350-$450
**Original, black hand:** . . . . . . . $450-$550
**Remake, m.o.c.:** . . . . . . . . . . $10-$15

*Original black Psychedelic Hand variation.*
**$450-$550**

*Original Psychedelic Hand dispensers.* **$350-$450**

*Comparison of the original dispenser* (**L**) *and the remake.*

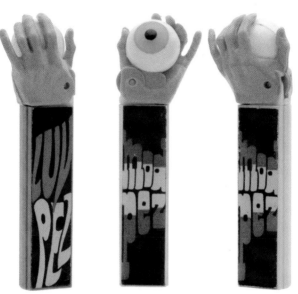

*A grouping of original Psychedelic Hands.* **$350-$450**

*A grouping of black Psychedelic hands.* **$450-$550**

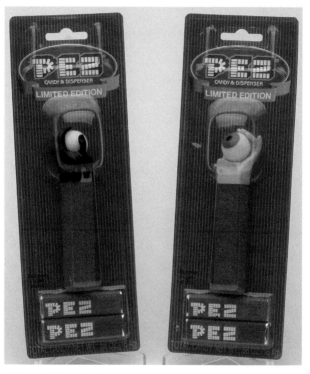

*Collector's Edition Hand on card—offered by PEZ® in 1998 through a mail-in offer.* **$10-$15**

### Raven

Early 1970s, no feet and with feet
Two versions were made of the Raven—
one with a short beak and one with a long
beak. The beak can be found in either
yellow or red. The long beak was not
released in the U.S. and usually sells for
about twice that of the regular version.

**Short beak, no feet:** ........ $75-$90
**Short beak, feet:** .......... $50-$75
**Long beak:** ............... $150-$200

*Yellow short beak no feet version of Raven.*
*$75-$90*

*Yellow long beak version of Raven.* **$150-$200**
*(Long beak from the Maryann Kennedy collection.)*

*Red short beak with feet version of Raven* **(L)** **$50-$75,**
*and long beak version.* **$150-$200**
*(Long beak from the Maryann Kennedy collection.)*

## Regular, Advertising

These dispensers were never mass-produced.
Most were screened one at a time and in very
small quantities. They were given to customers
and sales reps as "business cards." Ad Regulars
are very difficult to find, and from time to time
previously unknown ads turn up. The ultra-rare
"Lonicot" regular is among the rarest of the
Advertising dispensers. Only two are currently
known to exist. Lonicot is German for "low
nicotine." PEZ® was touted as an alternative to
smoking, so for a brief time they experimented
with a candy that actually contained nicotine.
This is the container that was to dispense that
candy. To this date no candy has been found,
only the dispenser and a small bit of paperwork.

Value: . . . . . . . . . . . . . . . . . . **$1000-$1500 each**
Lonicot dispenser: . . . . . . . . . **$3000+**

*Safeway ad regular.* **$1000-$1500**
*(From the Johann Patek collection.)*

*The ultra-rare "Lonicot" regular.* **$3000+**
*(From the Maryann Kennedy collection.)*

*Bosch ad regulars.* **$1000-$1500**
*( From the Johann Patek collection. )*

*Box Patent regular (non U.S.). A very rare dispenser.* **$4000+**
*(From the Maryann Kennedy collection.)*

## Regular, Box Patent

Early 1950s

This is believed to be the second-generation dispenser design, the box trademark being the first. It was not sold in the U.S. and is a very rare dispenser.

**Value:** ................. **$4000+**

### Regular, Box Trademark
Late 1940s to early 1950s
Thought to be the first generation of
dispenser design.
**Value: . . . . . . . . . . . . . . . . . $4500+**

*Box Trademark regular.* **$4500+**
*(From the Johann Patek collection.)*

### Regular, Locking Cap
Late 1940s
**Value:** . . . . . . . . . . . . . . . . . **$4000+**

*Rare Locking Cap regular.* **$4000+**
*(From the Johann Patek collection.)*

*Comparison of a new regular (**L**), and a vintage regular.*

## Regular, New
Mid-1990s
A new line of Regulars were produced in the 1990s, but with a
noticeable difference in the cap. There is also a new line of Regulars
with different colors that are only available in Japan.
**New U.S. regulars: . . . . . . . . . $3-$5**

## New Japan regulars
**Pink, white, or gray: . . . . . . . . $5-$10**
**Gold: . . . . . . . . . . . . . . . . . $30-$40**
**Black: . . . . . . . . . . . . . . . . . $15-$20**

*Rare long gray regular and "Klick and Spend" ad regular.* **$NA**
*(From the Johann Patek collection.)*

*Newer regulars with matching inner sleeves.*
*These are known as "mono regulars."* **$NA**
*(From the Johann Patek collection.)*

*Current line of U.S. regulars.* **$3-$5**

*More color variations of the current line of U.S. regulars.* **$3-$5**

*The only known original PEZ® regular.* $NA
*(From the Johann Patek collection.)*

## Regular, Original

Here it is, the ORIGINAL PEZ® regular! This little guy is just over 3/4-inch wide and barely measures 2-1/2-inches tall. It matches the size of the mechanical drawing for patent number 2,620,061 exactly!

*The opposite side.*

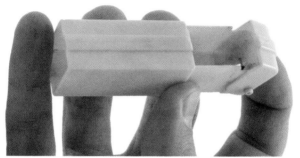

*With the sleeve extended.*

### Regular, Vintage
1950s
There are many different cap/stem color combinations including some that are semi-transparent through which you can see the inner workings of the dispenser.

**Value:** . . . . . . . . . . . . . . . . . . **$100-$150**

*Disposable vintage regular.* **$100-$150**

*Vintage regulars with "personalized" variations.*
*(From the Johann Patek collection.)*

*More vintage regulars with "personalized" variations.*
*(From the Johann Patek collection.)*

*Vintage regulars.* **$100-$150**
*(From the Johann Patek collection.)*

*Vintage regulars.* **$100-$150**
*(From the Johann Patek collection.)*

*Vintage regulars.* **$100-$150**
*(From the Johann Patek collection.)*

*Vintage regulars.* **$100-$150**
*(From the Johann Patek collection.)*

*Vintage regulars.* **$100-$150**
*(From the Johann Patek collection.)*

### Regular, Witch
Mid-1950s
This is among the rarest of PEZ® dispensers.
A picture of a witch is screened on both sides
of the stem.
**Value:** . . . . . . . . . . . . . . . . . . **$3500+**

*Light orange Witch regular.* **$3500+**
*(From the Johann Patek collection.)*

*Dark orange Witch regular.* **$3500+**
*(From the Johann Patek collection.)*

## Rhino (whistle)
No feet and with feet

**No feet:** ................. **$15-$25**
**With feet:** ............... **$5-$10**

*Rhino, whistle with feet.* **$5-$10**

**Ringmaster**
Mid-1970s, no feet
An uncommon dispenser—and usually
found missing his moustache.
**Value:** . . . . . . . . . . . . . . . . . **$275-$350**

*Ringmaster.* **$275-$350**

### Roadrunner

Early 1980s, no feet and with feet

**Painted eyes, no feet:** . . . . . . . **$30-$40**
**Painted eyes, with feet:** . . . . . **$25-$30**
**Stencil eyes, with feet (this is the most common version):** . . . . . . . . . **$20-$25**

*Roadrunner, stencil eyes with feet.* **$20-$25**

*Roadrunner, painted eyes with feet* (L)
*$25-$30, and painted eyes no feet* (R). *$30-$40*

*Very rare gold robot.* **$2000+**
*(From the Johann Patek collection.)*

## Robot (Also known as the Spacetrooper)

1950s

This is one of two "full body" dispensers. They stand approximately 3-1/2" tall and have the letters "PEZ" on their back. They are tough to find.

**Red or blue:** . . . . . . . . . . . . . $350-$450
**Yellow or dark blue:** . . . . . . . . $300-$400
**Shiny gold (very rare):** . . . . . . $2000+

*Robot, red.* $350-$450

*Robot, blue* **(L)** *$350-$450, and dark blue* **(R).** *$300-$400*

*Robot, yellow.* **$300-$400**

## Rooster

Mid-1970s, no feet
There are several different color
variations with white being the most
common followed by yellow and green.

**White:** . . . . . . . . . . . . . . . . . $40-$50
**Yellow or green:** . . . . . . . . . . $65-$85

*Rooster, green head.* **$65-$85**
*(From the Maryann Kennedy collection.)*

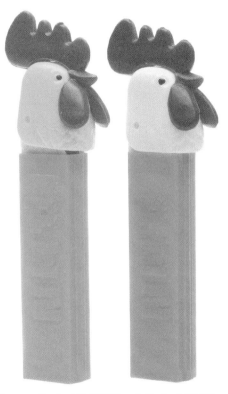

*Rooster, yellow head* **(L)** *$65-$85, and white head.* *$40-$50*

### Rooster (whistle)
No feet and with feet

**No feet:** . . . . . . . . . . . . . . . . $35-$45
**With feet:** . . . . . . . . . . . . . $25-$35

*Rooster, whistle with feet.* $25-$35

*Rudolph, no feet.* **$50-$75**

## Rudolph

Late 1970s, no feet and with feet
The mold used to produce Bambi was
also used for Rudolph—but the nose on
Rudolph was painted red.

**No feet:** . . . . . . . . . . . . . . . . . **$50-$75**
**With feet:** . . . . . . . . . . . . . . **$35-$50**

### Sailor
Late 1960s, no feet
**Value:** . . . . . . . . . . . . . . . . . . **$175-$225**

*Sailor.* **$175-$225**

*Santa, version A* **(L)** *$120-$150, B version* **(R)**. *$125-$160*

## Santa

1950s to Present, no feet and with feet

Santa is one of the most popular PEZ® dispensers ever produced. Most commonly found is Santa C, which has been produced since the 1970s.

**Santa A, no feet, face and beard are the same color:**
...................... **$120-$150**
**Santa B, no feet, flesh-colored face with white beard:**
...................... **$125-$160**
**Santa C, no feet:** ......... **$5-$10**
**Santa C, with**
**loop for ornament:** ........ **$35-$50**
**Santa C, with feet:** ........ **$2-$3**
**Santa D, with feet:** ........ **$1-$2**
**Santa E, (current):**.......... **$1-$2**
**Full body Santa (1950s):** ..... **$150-$200**

*Full Body Santa.* **$150-$200**

*Santa, version C with feet,* **$2-$3**, *and version D.* **$1-$2**

## Scrooge McDuck

Late 1970s, no feet and with feet
The original version used the same mold
that was used for Donald Duck version
B, with the glasses, sideburns and hat as
separately molded pieces (and easily lost).
The remake version has molded sideburns.

**Original, no feet:** .......... $30-$40
**Original, with feet:** ......... $25-$35
**Remake version:** .......... $5-$8

*Scrooge McDuck, original no feet.* **$30-$40**

*Scrooge McDuck, remake version.* **$5-$8**

## Sheik

Early 1970s, no feet
The Sheik can be found with either a red
or black band on top of the burnoose.

**Red band:** . . . . . . . . . . . . . . **$80-$100**
**Black band:** . . . . . . . . . . . . . . **$90-$125**

*Sheik, red band.* **$80-$100**

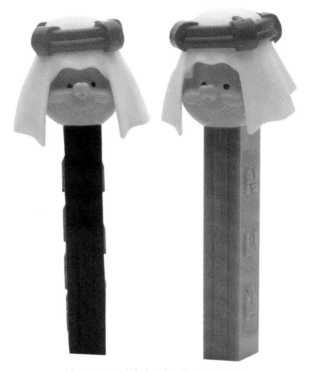

*More versions of Sheik with red band.* **$80-$100**

### Sheriff
Late 1970s, no feet
**Value:** . . . . . . . . . . . . . . . . . . $150-$200

*Sheriff.* **$150-$200**

**Silver Glow**
Early 1990s
**Value:** . . . . . . . . . . . . . . . . . $25-$40

*Silver Glow.* **$25-$40**

## Simpsons

Spring 2000, with feet

Doh! It's the whole Simpson family! Marge, Homer, Bart, Lisa, and Maggie.

**Value:** . . . . . . . . . . . . . . . . . **$1-$2 each**

*Bart Simpson.* **$1-$2**

*Maggie, Lisa, Homer, and Marge Simpson.* **$1-$2**

*Rare marbleized Skull variations.* **$NA**
*(From the Johann Patek collection.)*

## Skull

Early 1970s to current, no feet and with feet

A "misfit" version of the skull with a black head was available in 1998 through a mail-in offer. A very hard-to-find variation of version B is known as the "Colgate" skull, because he has a full set of teeth!

| | |
|---|---|
| **Version A, no feet:** . . . . . . . . | $15-$20 |
| **Version A, with feet:** . . . . . . . . | $10-$15 |
| **Version B, larger head:** . . . . . . | $1-$3 |
| **Version B, glows in the dark:** . . | $1-$3 |
| **"Misfit" version:** . . . . . . . . . . | $5-$8 |
| **Full set of teeth:** . . . . . . . . . . . | $50-$60 |

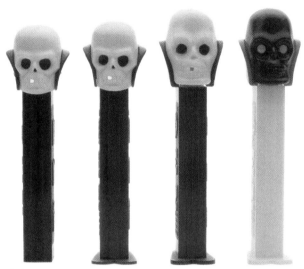

*Skull, (L to R) version A no feet $15-$20, version A with feet $10-$15, version B with larger head $1-$3, and Misfit version. $5-$8*

### Smiley

Have a nice day! It's the smiley face dispenser, found only at Wal-Mart, this guy can be found on purple, green, orange, blue, or yellow stems.

**Value:** . . . . . . . . . . . . . . . . . . **$1-$3**

*Smiley.* **$1-$3**

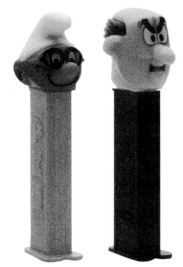

*Brainy Smurf and Gargamel, second series.* **$3-$5**

## Smurfs

Late 1980s, no feet and with feet

Two Smurf series were produced—one in the late 1980s and the second in the late 1990s. Series one included Smurf, Smurfette, and Papa Smurf. The second series includes Smurf, Papa Smurf, Smurfette, Brainy Smurf, and Gargamel.

**Smurf (first series):** ........ **$10-$15**
**Smurfette (first series):** ...... **$10-$15**
**Papa Smurf (first series):** .... **$10-$15**
**Second series:** ........... **$3-$5 each**

*Second series Smurf, Papa Smurf, and Smurfette.* **$3-$5**

*Smurfs, original series, including Smurf, Papa Smurf, and Smurfette with feet*
**$5-$10**, *and no feet.* **$10-$15**

## Snow White

Late 1960s, no feet
Collar color variations include white,
yellow, turquoise, and green. Turquoise is
worth slightly more.
**Value:** .................. **$200-$225**

*Snow White.* **$200-$225**
*(From the Maryann Kennedy collection.)*

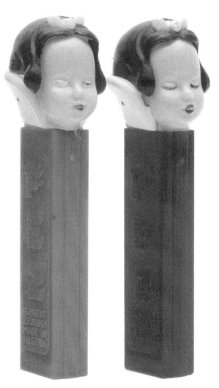

*Additional color variations of Snow White.* **$200-$225**

**Warman's PEZ Field Guide**

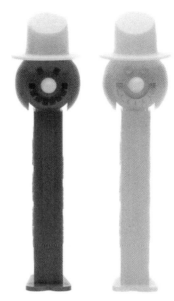

*Snowman, "misfit" versions.* **$5-$8**

## Snowman

1970s, no feet and with feet

**No feet: . . . . . . . . . . . . . . . . . $15-$25**
**With feet: . . . . . . . . . . . . . . . $1-$5**
**"Misfit" versions**
**(mail-in offer, late 1990s): . . . $5-$8**

*Snowman, no feet* $15-$25, *and with feet.* $1-$5

## Softhead Superheroes
Late 1970s, no feet
The heads on these dispensers are made of a
soft eraser-like material and usually found only
on USA marked stems. These are very popular
with collectors. Characters in the series
include: Batman, Penguin, Wonder Woman,
Joker, and Batgirl.
**Value:** . . . . . . . . . . . . . . . . . **$150-$200 each**

*Batman Softhead Superhero.* **$150-$200**

*Penguin and Wonder Woman Softhead Superheroes.* **$150-$200**

*Joker and Batgirl Softhead Superheroes.* $150-$200

## Sourz

Released summer of 2002. Pineapple, Blue
Raspberry, Watermelon, and Green Apple
come with new sour PEZ® candy!
**Value: . . . . . . . . . . . . . . . . . . $1-$2 each**

*Sourz Pineapple.* $1-$2

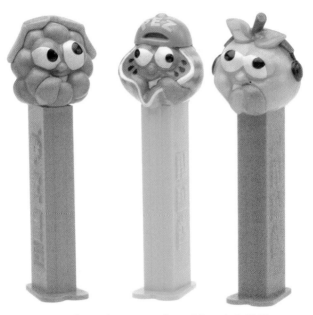

*Sourz Blue Raspberry, Watermelon, and Green Apple.* **$1-$2**

## Spaceman
Late 1950s, no feet

A premium version of the Spaceman was offered by Cocoa Marsh in the late 1950s. The premium version had "Cocoa Marsh" on the stem. Several stem variations include light blue, dark blue, and metallic blue, as well as clear or transparent blue helmet.

**Value:** . . . . . . . . . . . . . . . . . $150-$175
**Cocoa Marsh Spaceman:** . . . . . $175-$225

*Cocoa Marsh Spaceman.* **$175-$225**

*Spaceman dispenser, from the late 1950s. Same as Cocoa Marsh Spaceman,
except this one has the PEZ® logo on both sides.* **$150-$175**

## Sparefroh

Early 1970s, no feet

"Sparefroh" is German for "happy saver."
October 31st of each year in Europe is World
Savings Day when all people are encouraged
to save money in a bank. (Thus the tie-in with
the coin that is glued to the front of the stem)
This was a gift to children who put money
in their bank account on that day. There are
two different stem inscriptions: "110 Jahre
Allgemeine Sparkasse in Linz" and "Deine
Sparkasse." The dispenser must have the coin
attached to be considered complete.

**Value:** . . . . . . . . . . . . . . . . **$1200-$1500**

*Sparefroh.* $1200-$1500

### Speedy Gonzales
Late 1970s to current, no feet and with feet

**No feet:** . . . . . . . . . . . . . . . . . $30-$40
**With feet, older head:** . . . . . . . $15-$25
**Current:** . . . . . . . . . . . . . . . . $1-$2

*Speedy Gonzales, current version.* **$1-$2**

*Spider-Man, Late 1970s with feet* **$5-$8**, *and no feet.* **$15-$20**

## Spider-Man

Late 1970s, no feet and with feet
Several versions of Spider-Man have been produced.

**Smaller head, no feet:** ...... **$15-$20**
**Medium size head, with feet:** .. **$5-$8**
**Larger head, with feet (current): $1-$2**

## Spike
Early 1980s, no feet and with feet
Spike was not released in the U.S. Several
versions exist including small painted eyes,
decal eyes and an unusual variation with a
green head.

**Decal eyes:** . . . . . . . . . . . . . . $5-$10
**Small painted eyes:** . . . . . . . . $15-$20
**Green head:** . . . . . . . . . . . . $100-$125

*Spike, decal eyes.* **$5-$10**

*Spike, small painted eyes.* **$15-$20**

## Star Wars

Late 1990s, with feet

PEZ® released three series of dispensers featuring characters from the Star Wars universe. The first series included five dispensers: Darth Vader, Stormtrooper, C3-PO, Yoda, and Chewbacca. The second series, released summer of 1999 included: Ewok, Princess Leia, Boba Fett, and Luke Skywalker. The third series released summer 2002 in conjunction with the movie Attack of the Clones featured Jango Fett, R2-D2, and Clone Trooper.

**Value (all series):** . . . . . . . . . **$1-$3 each**

*Jango Fett.* **$1-$3**

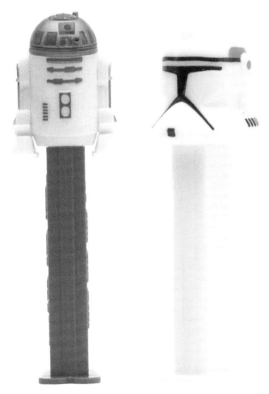

*R2-D2 and Clone Trooper.* **$1-$3**

*Sylvester, two variations of current version.* **$1-$2**

## Sylvester

Late 1970s, no feet and with feet
Several versions of Tweety Bird's nemesis exist.

**No feet:** . . . . . . . . . . . . . . . . **$15-$20**
**With feet, older style head:** . . . **$5-$8**
**With feet, with whiskers (black lines
under nose), non-U.S. version:** **$4-$8**
**Currents:** . . . . . . . . . . . . . . . **$1-$2**

*Sylvester, no feet $15-$20, with feet and older-style head $5-$8, and with feet and whiskers. $4-$8*

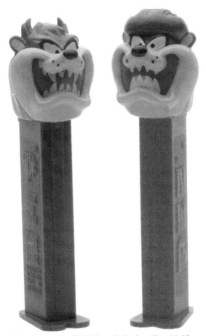

*Tazmanian Devil* **$1-$2**, *and Cycling Taz.* **$1-$2**

## Tazmanian Devil
Late 1990s, with feet

**Value:** ................ **$1-$2**
**Cycling Taz (with hat)** ....... **$1-$2**

### Teenage Mutant Ninja Turtles

Mid-1990s, with feet

Two series were produced—a smiling version and an angry version of Leonardo, Michaelangelo, Donatello, and Raphael. With 8 different turtle heads and 8 stem colors, collecting all variations presents a bit of a challenge.

**Smiling version:** . . . . . . . . . . . **$2-$3 each**
**Angry version:** . . . . . . . . . . . . **$2-$3 each**

*Teenage Mutant Ninja Turtles, Leonardo smiling version.* **$2-$3**

*Teenage Mutant Ninja Turtles, angry version Leonardo, Raphael, Donatello, and Michaelangelo.* **$2-$3**

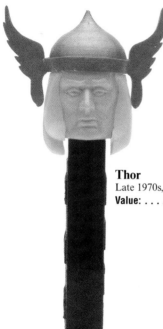

## Thor
Late 1970s, no feet
**Value:** .................... **$250-$300**

*Thor.* **$250-$300**

### Thumper
Late 1970s, no feet and with feet
A very subtle yet pricey variation of this dispenser has the copyright symbol along with the letters "WDP" on the head.

**No feet, no copyright:** ....... **$85-$100**
**With feet:** ................ **$60-$80**
**With copyright:** .......... **$200+**

*Thumper, with feet.* **$60-$80**

**Tiger**
With feet
**Value:** . . . . . . . . . . . . . . . . . . $5-$10

*Tiger, whistle.* $5-$10

*Tinkerbell.* **$200-$250**

## Tinkerbell
Late 1960s, no feet
**Value: . . . . . . . . . . . . . . . . . $200-$250**

*Tom, with feet* **(L & C)** *$3-$8, and multi-piece face ( R).* **$5-$10**

## Tom

Early 1980s, No feet and with feet
The feline portion of MGM's famous cat and mouse pair. Not released in the U.S. Several versions have been produced.

**No feet:** . . . . . . . . . . . . . . . . . $25-$35
**With feet:** . . . . . . . . . . . . . . . $3-$8
**Multi-piece face:** . . . . . . . . . $5-$10

*Tom, no feet* **(L)** *$25-$35, and with feet.* **$3-$8**

### Tuffy
Early 1990s, with feet
A non-U.S. release, Tuffy looks very
similar to Jerry, but has gray face instead
of brown.

**Painted face:** . . . . . . . . . . . . . . $3-$5
**Multi-piece face:** . . . . . . . . . $10-$15
**Current:** . . . . . . . . . . . . . . . . $2-$4

*Tuffy, multi-piece face.* **$10-$15**

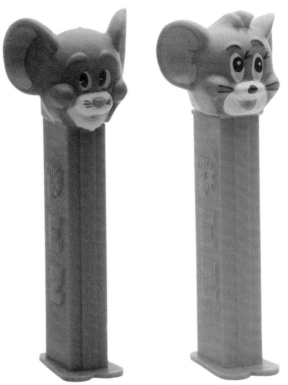

*Tuffy, painted face* **(L)** *$3-$5, and current.* *$2-$4*

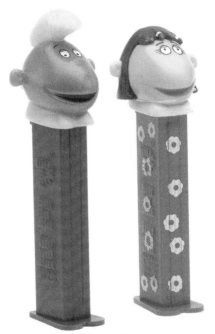

*Tweenies, Jake and Fizz.* **$2-$4**

## Tweenies
2002, with feet
Released in Europe summer of 2002.
**Value:** .................. **$2-$4 each**

*Tweenies, (**L to R**) Milo, Bella, and Doodles. $2-$4*

### Tweety

Late 1970s to current, no feet and with feet
The oldest version is hardest to find; it
has separate pieces for the eyes (known as
removable eyes).

**Removable eyes, no feet:** .... $20-$25
**Painted eyes, no feet:** ....... $15-$20
**Painted eyes, with feet:** ..... $3-$5
**Current:** ................ $1-$2

*Tweety, removable eyes.* **$20-$25**

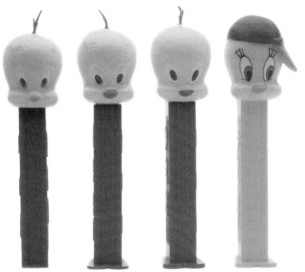

*Tweety,* **(L to R)** *painted eyes no feet* **$15-$20***, painted eyes with feet* **$3-$5***, and current version.* **$1-$2**

### Tyke

Early 1980s, no feet and with feet
Non-U.S. release.
**Small painted eyes:** ........ $25-$35
**Decal eyes:** ............. $15-$20

*Tyke, small painted eyes.* **$25-$35**

*Tyke, decal eyes.* $15-$20

*Uncle Sam.* **$175-$200**

## Uncle Sam
Mid-1970s, no feet
**Value:** . . . . . . . . . . . . . . . . . . **$175-$200**

## Universal Studios Monsters
Mid-1960s, no feet
A highly coveted series among PEZ®
collectors and Universal Studio fans. The
Creature has a very unique pearlescent
stem.

**Creature from
the Black Lagoon:** ......... $300-$350
**Wolfman:** ............... $275-$325
**Frankenstein:** ........... $275-$325

*Universal Studios Monsters,
Wolfman.* **$275-$325**

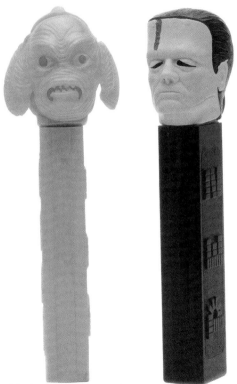

*Universal Studios Monsters, Creature from the Black Lagoon* **$300-$350**, *and Frankenstein.* **$275-$325**

### USA Hearts
2002 mail-in offer. A set of six was offered for $8.95
**Value:** .................. **$8.95**

*USA Hearts.* **$8.95**

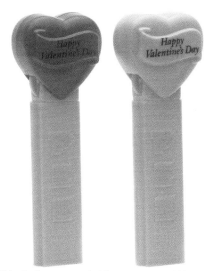

*Valentine hearts, unusual pink stem variations.* **$125-$150**

## Valentine

1970s to current, no feet and with feet

**Boy and Girl PEZ® Pals on die-cut Valentine cards, no feet, 1970s:**
. . . . . . . . . . . . . . . . . . . . . . $150-$200 each
**Boy and Girl PEZ® Pals on Valentine cards, with feet, late 1980s/early 1990s:** . . . . . . . . . . . . . . . . . $15-$20 each
**Valentine hearts,**
**red stem, no feet:** . . . . . . . . $1-$3
**Valentine hearts, unusual**
**pink stem, no feet:** . . . . . . . . $125-$150

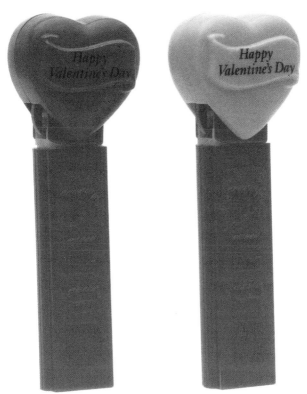

*Valentine hearts, red stems.* **$1-$3**

*Boy and Girl on die-cut Valentine cards from the 1970s.*

*Boy and Girl on Valentine cards from the 1980s-early 1990s.*

### Wile E. Coyote

Early 1980s, no feet and with feet

**No feet:** . . . . . . . . . . . . . . . . . $45-$65
**With feet:** . . . . . . . . . . . . . . . $35-$45

*Wile E. Coyote, with feet.* **$35-$45**

## Winnie the Pooh

Late 1970s, no feet and with feet
This dispenser was initially released only
in Europe. Winnie the Pooh has been
quite popular among collectors in general,
causing his price to more than double the
last few years. Remade and re-released in
the summer of 2001, Winnie the Pooh and
friends can now be found in the U.S.

**No feet:** . . . . . . . . . . . . . . . . **$75-$100**
**With feet:** . . . . . . . . . . . . . . . **$65-$85**
**Remakes:**. . . . . . . . . . . . . . . . **$1-$3**

*1970s Winnie the Pooh, with feet.* **$65-$85**

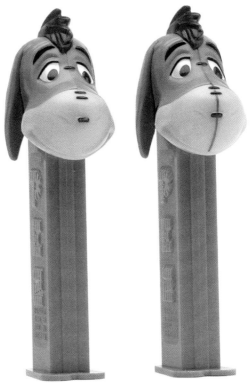

*Winnie the Pooh remakes, Eeoyore, the version on the right with the line down his nose is the first version and is harder to find.* **$1-$3**

*Winnie the Pooh remakes, Pooh, Piglet, and Tigger.* **$1-$3**

*Witch, A version.* **$200-$250**

## Witch

Late 1950s to current, no feet and with feet

Witch A, orange head,
no feet, 1950s: . . . . . . . . . . . $200-$250
Witch B, orange head, slightly taller hat than A, no feet:
. . . . . . . . . . . . . . . . . . . . . . $2000+
Three-piece Witch,
no feet, 1970s: . . . . . . . . . . . $20-$30
Three-piece Witch, no feet, unusual color combinations:
. . . . . . . . . . . . . . . . . . . . . . $100-$150
Three-piece Witch, with feet: . . $3-$5
Witch C: . . . . . . . . . . . . . . . . $1-$2
Witch C, glow in the
dark version (current): . . . . . . . $1-$2
"Misfit" version (late 1990s): . $5-$8
"Convention witch": . . . . . . . . $30-$40

*Witch, rare B version.* **$2000+**
*(From the Adam Young collection.)*

*Glow-in–the-dark Witch, convention version.* **$30-$40**

*Unusual three-piece Witch variations.* **$100-$150**
*(From the Johann Patek collection.)*

*More unusual three-piece Witch variations.* **$100-$150**
*(From the Maryann Kennedy collection.)*

*More unusual three-piece Witch variations.* **$100-$150**
*(From the Maryann Kennedy collection.)*

*Wolverine.* **$1-$2**

## Wolverine
1999, with feet
This is one of the characters from the popular X-Men comic.
**Value:** . . . . . . . . . . . . . . . . . . . **$1-$2**

## Wonder Woman

Late 1970s, no feet and with feet
Two versions of Wonder Woman were
produced—the earlier has a raised star on
her headband while on the second version
the star is flat.

**Raised star, no feet:** . . . . . . . $20-$25
**Raised star, with feet:** . . . . . . $5-$10
**Flat star, with feet (current):** . . $1-$2

*Wonder Woman, raised star with feet.* **$5-$10**

*Wonder Woman, flat star.* **$1-$2**

*Unusual Wonder Woman test molds.* **$NA**
*(From the Johann Patek collection.)*

**Wounded Soldier**
Mid-1970s, no feet
**Value:** . . . . . . . . . . . . . . . . . $125-$150

*Wounded Soldier.* $125-$150

### Yosemite Sam
Mid 1990s, with feet
The shorter mustache on the non-U.S.
version allows body parts to be put on the
dispenser.
**U.S. version:** . . . . . . . . . . . . . **$1-$2**
**Non-U.S. version:** . . . . . . . . **$2-$4**

*Yosemite Sam, U.S. version.* **$1-$2**

*Yosemite Sam, non-U.S. version.* $2-$4

## Zorro

1960s, no feet

This dispenser can be found in several different versions: small and large logo and variations of the hat and mask. Some versions have a curved mask and others have a straight mask.

**Versions with logo:** . . . . . . . . . **$100-$125**
**Non-logo:** . . . . . . . . . . . . . . **$75-$100**

*Zorro, non-logo.* $75-$100

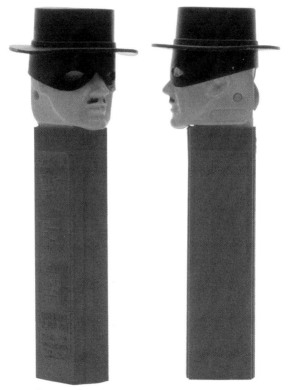

*Zorro, non-logo* **(L)** $75-$100, *logo version* **(R)**. $100-$125

# ILLUSTRATED GLOSSARY

## BUTTON

**BUTTON:** An opaque rectangle piece inside the stem, usually red but sometimes white, that the candy actually sits on. There are a couple versions: a rectangle with square corners, and a rectangle with rounded corners. The square corner version is the oldest.

# CHANNEL

**CHANNEL:** The groove on the front of the dispenser that runs the length of the stem.

## CLUB MED

**CLUB MED:** A term used when a character's face appears very tan, as if they have been in the sun or at Club Med. This can also be considered a color variation.

# COLOR VARIATION

**COLOR VARIATION:** Refers to the comparison of like dispensers in which one has a different color to the entire head or to one or more of the parts found on the head. Example: a cow may have a head that is yellow, blue, orange, green, etc. The possibilities are almost infinite.

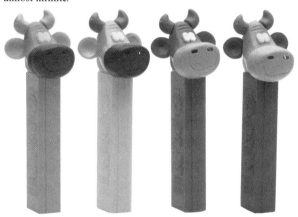

## DBP

**DBP:** The German patent number on a dispenser. It means "Deutsches Bundes Patent" and will be accompanied by the numbers 818 829.

## FEET

*This is one of only a few examples of an early-footed dispenser known to exist.*

*(From the Maryann Kennedy collection.)*

**FEET:** Small rounded plastic protrusions or tabs at the base of the stem to help the dispenser stand upright. Feet were added to dispensers in the U.S. around 1987. Currently there are 2 different styles. The earlier version is known as "thin feet," referring to the fact that the plastic of the feet is not as thick as the plastic feet found on current dispensers. Beware, some people try to cut the feet off and pass them off as a footless dispenser. Some dispensers were produced both ways, with feet and without. Look to the spine of the stem to tell if it has been altered.

## HEAD & IMC

**HEAD:** The top-most part of the dispenser that tilts back to dispense the candy.

**IMC:** Injection Mold Code. A single digit number found on the outside top corner of the stem. Identifies in which plastic factory the dispenser was molded. Not all dispensers have IMC's. Here is a list to help identify which number goes with which country:
1 & 3: Austria/ Hungary
2: Austria/ Hong Kong
4 & 8: Austria
5: Yugoslavia/ Slovenia
6: Hong Kong/ China
7: Hong Kong/ Austria/ Czech Republic
9: U.S.A.
V: Yugoslavia (changed to Slovenia in 1993)

## KICKER

**KICKER:** Sometimes referred to as the "pusher," this is the small plastic piece that extends down from the back of the head and pushes out a single piece of candy when the head is tilted back.

*Blade-type spring (**L**) and classic wire mechanism (**R**). The kicker is shown just below the spring.*

## LOOSE & MARBLEIZED

**LOOSE:** the dispenser is out of its original packaging.

**MARBLEIZED:** a term used when two or more colors of plastic are combined and not thoroughly mixed, causing a swirling pattern to appear in the finished product. This is a sought after variation by some collectors.

## MELT MARK, M.I.B, M.I.C, M.O.C, M.O.M.C & N/F

**MELT MARK:** refers to damage on the dispenser. Sometimes caused by direct heat or a chemical reaction between the plastic of the dispenser and certain types of rubber or other plastics. Certain types of rubber bands and items like rubber-fishing worms have been known to cause melt marks when left in contact with a dispenser.

**M.I.B.:** Mint In Bag. Bag will have colored ends and writing as well as the PEZ® logo. Newer style. Also known as a "poly bag."

**M.I.C.:** Mint In Cellophane or Mint In Cello. Bag will be clear with no writing.

**M.O.C.:** Mint On Card.

**M.O.M.C.:** Mint On Mint Card. Both dispenser and card are in pristine condition.

**N/F:** no feet.

# PATENT NUMBER

**PATENT NUMBER:** Seven digit number located on the side of the stem. Currently there are five different U.S. patent numbers on PEZ® dispensers: 2,620,061 is the earliest, followed by

*2.6 patent closeup with thin feet. This is a rare oddity.*

3,410,455; 3,845,882; 3,942,683 and 4,966,305. 3,370,746 was issued for the candy shooter and appears on the 1980s space gun as well. Patent numbers can help identify the age of a dispenser, but generally do not play a part in its value. Not all dispensers have a patent number on them, certain dispensers have no patent numbers, and this does not affect the value of those dispensers. Feet first started to appear on dispenser bases when the 3,942,683 number was issued, but some exceptions can be found with feet and earlier issue patent numbers. These dispensers are difficult to find and carry a little more value with some collectors.

## PEZHEAD & PIN

**PEZHEAD:** A term used to describe someone who collects PEZ®!

**PIN:** Steel pin that hinges the head. Made of metal and found only in older dispensers. The pin runs through the side of the head and the sleeve, attaching it to the dispenser base.

## REGULAR

**REGULAR:** The earliest PEZ® dispensers. These didn't have a character head; instead they had only a thumb grip at the top and were marketed for adults. These were remade in the late 1990s, but with a noticeable difference. Vintage regulars will have a raised thumb grip on the top of the cap. The remakes will have a square cap with no raised grip and the spine will be deeper than the channel.

*The dispenser at left is a re-make and the example shown at right is an original.*

**Illustrated Glossary**

# SHOES

*Original shoe shown on far left.*

**SHOES:** An accessory for your dispenser that fits on the base of the stem. Similar to feet in that its purpose is to give the dispenser more stability when standing upright. Originally made to be used with the Make-a-Face dispenser. Reproduction shoes have been made with a rounded toe in the front, and can be found in at least three colors: black, white, and red. There is also a reproduction glow-in-the-dark version. An original shoe will always be black and have a "B" shape to the end.

486        **Warman's PEZ Field Guide**

## SLEEVES

**SLEEVE:** The part of the dispenser that pulls out of the stem and holds the candy. The United States patent description refers to this part as the magazine.

## SOFTHEAD

**SOFTHEAD:** The head is made of a rubber, eraser-like material that is pliable and softer than traditional plastic head dispensers, hence the name "softhead." Softheads can be found in the Erie Specter and Superhero series, along with a very rare Disney set that never made it to mass production.

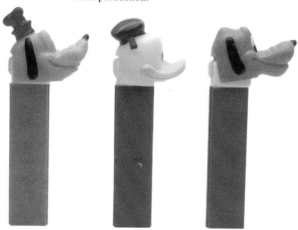

# SPINE

**SPINE:** The groove on the back of the dispenser that runs the length of the stem. On a vintage footless dispenser the spine should be the same depth as the channel. Some unscrupulous people will try to pass off a dispenser as footless by cutting off the feet and claiming that it is old. To detect tampering, turn the dispenser upside down and compare the spine to the channel. The spine on a footed dispenser will always be deeper than its channel.

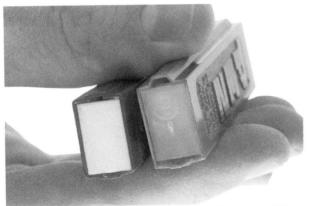

*Vintage footless dispenser* **(L)** *and footed dispenser with feet removed* **(R)**.

# SPRING

**SPRING:** Refers to either the spring inside the stem directly under the button, OR the spring in the top of the dispenser that keeps tension on the character head. There are three basic types of springs in the top of the dispenser: the classic wire mechanism, the blade spring, and currently a "leaf spring" mechanism.

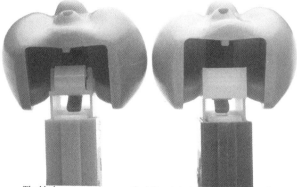

*The blade spring is shown on the left and the leaf spring on the right.*

## STEM, TRANSITION PIECE & W/F

**STEM:** The lower part of the dispenser. Usually has the PEZ® logo on at least one side and possibly country of origin, patent number, and injection mold code. Depending on the dispenser, the stem may also be die-cut or be completely smooth on one or both sides.

**TRANSITION PIECE:** A dispenser that has characteristics of a previous model, but also has features of a current dispenser. These pieces must still be in their original packaging to show they are void of alterations. Example: an old-style character head that is on a footed stem.

**W/F:** with feet.

# CONVENTIONS

Do you want to meet other collectors? Have lots of fun? See more PEZ® than you ever imagined? Attend a PEZ® convention! Conventions are one of the best ways to gain information and knowledge of the hobby, as well as to buy and sell PEZ®. You will find many rare and unusual items displayed, as well as organized events such as "Pez Bingo" to keep you busy.

Conventions have been sprouting up since the early 1990s, drawing people from all over the U.S and the world. Below you will find a current list of conventions, check PEZ Collectors News for exact times and dates.

1. **Southern California** – Conventions have been held since 1994 in several different locations with different hosts. Usually meets sometime in the spring.

2. **St. Louis, Missouri** – First convention held in 1993 and still going strong. Meets in June. Your host is John "CoolPezman" Devlin, who may be reached using the Web site, http:/www.pezconvention.com or the 24-hour hotline: (314) 416-0333.

3. **Bloomington, Minnesota** – First convention held in October 1996 across from the Mall of America. Now meets in August rather than October. Your hosts are Dana and Julie Kraft, they may be reached using the Web site, www.MNPEZCON.com

**4. Cleveland, Ohio** – First ever PEZ® convention, "Dispensor-O-Rama" held June, 1991 in Mentor, Ohio. Continues to meet each July in the Cleveland area. Your host is Jill Cohen and she may be reached using the Web site, www.pezmania.com or at the following phone number:

**PEZAMANIA**
*Phone: (216) 283-5993 before 10pm EST*

**5. Connecticut** – Called the "East Coast PEZ® Convention" first met in April 1999 in Orange, Connecticut (home of PEZ® Candy, Inc.). Moved to a larger location in Stamford, CT for the May 2000 show. Your host is Richie Belyski (editor of PEZ Collectors News) and he may be reached using the Web site, www.pezcollectorsnews.com or at the following address:

**PEZ Collector's News**
*P.O. Box 14956*
*Surfside Beach, SC 29587*

# FINDING INFORMATION

Several newsletters have been dedicated to collecting PEZ®. The first, The Toy Candy Container and Food Premium Collector, appeared in 1987. With the third issue the name changed to The Old Variety Store. The OVS lasted until late 1989 and had a run of about 15 issues. In January 1990, the Optimistic Pezzimist came on board. It, too, had a run of just 15 issues, lasting until July of 1992. Without much delay, in the fall of 1992 the Positively Pez newsletter was started.

By this time the hobby was gaining steam. The first book about PEZ® had been released during the previous year, and collectors were becoming more knowledgeable than ever. Positively Pez had a run of 19 issues and ended with the January/February 1996 edition. With the announcement of its close, and with an ever-growing number of collectors hungry for the latest PEZ® information, two new publications were started. The Fliptop Pezervation Society premiered with the September/October 1995 issue, billing itself as "the first national club for PEZ® collectors." Pedro PEZ®, a boy PEZ® Pal dispenser, was adopted as the club mascot and was sent around the world with various collectors visiting interesting places and having his picture taken.

Right on the heels of the Fliptop newsletter, PEZ Collectors News made its first appearance with the October/November 1995 issue. The two newsletters worked well together, uniting collectors and giving them more information than ever before. In December 1999, the Fliptop Pezervation Society announced that the September/October 1999 issue was their last and they would combine efforts with PEZ Collectors News. FPS enjoyed a run of 24 issues. Currently PEZ Collectors News, put out bimonthly by Richie Belyski, is the only newsletter devoted to PEZ®. You can contact them at:

**PEZ Collector's News**
*P.O. Box 14956*
*Surfside Beach, SC 29587*
*E-mail: info@pezcollectorsnews.com*
*http://www.pezcollectorsnews.com*

# PEZ® IN SPACE

PEZ® in Space? Cyberspace, that is. A ton of information about PEZ® can be found on the Internet. It is an excellent source for up-to-date information and a great way to buy and sell PEZ®. There are hundreds, maybe even thousands, of sites built by collectors that detail everything from how to properly load your dispenser to pictures of personal collections.

One of the nicest collector-built sites is Pez Central. Good design, great graphics and pictures, up-to-date information, and links to other Web pages make it a great place to visit. Check it out at: www.pezcentral.com.

By now there are probably very few people who haven't heard of eBay. But did you know that eBay got its start with PEZ®? Pierre Omidyar, founder of eBay, originally created the site as a way for his girlfriend to buy and sell PEZ®

dispensers. To accomplish this, Omidyar built an Internet auction site that brought buyer and seller together on a level playing field. In doing so he created one of the most popular and fastest growing places on the Internet. There are now three PEZ® categories—General, Current, and Vintage—which offer an average of more than 3,000 items a week. You can find the site at: www.ebay.com.

PEZ® Candy, Inc. also has a Web site. Within their site you will find a FAQ list (Frequently Asked Questions), a list of PEZ® Dispensers offered to date in the United States, a list of other cool PEZ® products, information about PEZ® newsletters, and the PEZ® Store. The store sells many current dispensers and candy flavors, including some items that are unique and only available through the special mail-order program. The site can be found at: www.pez.com.

## STARTING UP

If you are a new collector you are probably wondering how to get started. Start out slowly—look for all of the current release dispensers you can find around your town. That alone will give you a nice size collection on which to build without spending too much money. Most collectors ask the questions: "Should I leave it in the package or open it up?" and "Will it loose its value if I open it?" Opening the dispenser is a matter of preference. If the dispenser is old, I would advise against opening the package. With the new stuff, it's up to you. Personally, I buy at least three of each new release; one in the bag, one on the card to save, and one to open for display. It's true, a carded or bagged dispenser is traditionally worth more than one that is loose, but a dispenser out of package is more fun to display.

Next, move on to the current European dispensers. Most of these can be had for $3 to $4 each. Acquire all of these and the size of your collection will almost double. When it comes to vintage dispensers, decide what your first "price plateau" will be and start from there. For example, there are still a good number of footless dispensers that can be found for $25 or less. Once you buy all of these, move on to the next price level and so on.

Although some of the old dispensers reach into the hundreds and even thousands of dollars, you don't have to spend your life savings to enjoy the hobby. Some collectors specialize and focus on collecting one favorite area such as the Animals or PEZ® Pal series. Others focus on stems by collecting a character that is made in several different countries, or by collecting as many different colors as they can. A good example of this is the Teenage Mutant Ninja Turtles. There are eight different dispensers that come on eight different stem colors, if you were to collect all of the combinations you would have 64 turtles alone in your collection!

The most important thing to remember about collecting PEZ®... it's a hobby—have fun!

# TRIVIA

*See page 500 for trivia question answers.*
**1)** *How many pieces of candy are in a regular pack of Pez candy?*

**2)** *Who invented the first PEZ dispenser?*

3) *PEZ is an acronym for what word?*

**4)** *Which dispenser is the all time best seller?*

**5)** *What do buttons, kickers, channels, sleeves, and feet all have in common?*

**6)** *In what U.S. city and state does PEZ call home?*

**7)** *What was the first dispenser to have the entire body on top of the dispenser?*

**8)** *Yappy dog can be found in several color variations, what other dispenser was created using the same head?*

**9)** *Name the two dispensers that can be found with a loop on the top of their head so they could also be used as a Christmas ornament?*

**10)** *Which dispenser was once used to promote chocolate-flavored syrup?*

**11)** *The prized Bride and Groom dispensers were originally created as place settings for who's wedding?*

**12)** *In what year did PEZ celebrate their 50th anniversary in the United States?*

**13)** *Who was the first sports team to have a PEZ dispenser promotion?*

**14)** *How many different flavors of PEZ candy are currently sold in the U.S.?*

**15)** *How many U.S. Presidents have appeared on the top of a PEZ dispenser?*

**16)** *Which dispenser was re-made to celebrate the company's 50th anniversary?*

**17)** *When and where did PEZ get its start?*

**18)** *When and where was the first ever PEZ convention?*

**19)** *Which dispenser became the focus of an episode on the popular television show Seinfeld?*

**20)** *What was the original price of a PEZ dispenser baseball set back in the 60s?*

**21)** *What flavor candy originally came with the psychedelic hand dispenser?*

**22)** *What flavor candy was never actually produced by PEZ—Chlorophyll, Eucalyptus, Licorice, Coffee, Blackberry, or Anise?*

**23)** *What is the name of the PEZ mascot?*

**24)** *Which of these three restaurants has never done a PEZ promotion- White Castle, McDonalds, or Jack-in- the-Box?*

## ANSWERS

**1.** (12), **2.** (Oskar Uxa in 1949) (spelling for his name is correct), **3.** (pfefferminz- the German word for peppermint), **4.** (Santa Claus), **5.** (they are all parts of a PEZ dispenser), **6.** (Headquarters is based in Orange, CT.), **7.** (the Hippo was first (R2-D2 was 2nd and Scoop from Bob the Builder series was 3rd.), **8.** (Cow B), **9.** (Angel and Santa Claus), **10.** (the spaceman for Cocoa Marsh), **11.** (Robert and Claudia- Oct. 6th 1978), **12.** (2002), **13.** (Chicago Cubs- June 14th 2000), **14.** (10 -Lemon, orange, grape, strawberry, peppermint, cola, sour blue raspberry, sour green apple, and sour pineapple), **15.** (0), **16.** (Golden Glow- 2002), **17.** (1927 Vienna, Austria), **18.** (June 15th, 1991 in Mentor, Ohio), **19.** (Tweety Bird), **20.** (.39 cents then, now…. $600-$800), **21.** (flower), **22.** (Blackberry), **23.** (Peter Pez), **24.** (McDonalds)

# INDEX

# C

Engineer . . . . . . . . . . . . . . . . . . . . . . . . . . 175

# F

Fireman. . . . . . . . . . . . . . . . . . . . . . . .176-177
Fishman . . . . . . . . . . . . . . . . . . . . . . . .178-179
Flintstones . . . . . . . . . . . . . . . . . . . . . .180-181
Foghorn Leghorn . . . . . . . . . . . . . . . . . .182-183
Football Player . . . . . . . . . . . . . . . . . . .184-185
Frog. . . . . . . . . . . . . . . . . . . . . . . . . . . . 186

# G

Garfield. . . . . . . . . . . . . . . . . . . . . . . . .187-190
Giraffe. . . . . . . . . . . . . . . . . . . . . . . . . . 191
Girl . . . . . . . . . . . . . . . . . . . . . . . . . . . .192-193
Golden Glow . . . . . . . . . . . . . . . . . . . . .194-196
Goofy . . . . . . . . . . . . . . . . . . . . . . . . . .197-200
Gorilla. . . . . . . . . . . . . . . . . . . . . . . . . . 201
Green Hornet . . . . . . . . . . . . . . . . . . . . .202-204
Groom. . . . . . . . . . . . . . . . . . . . . . . . . . 205

# H

Halloween Crystal Series . . . . . . . . . . . . .206-207
Halloween Ghosts . . . . . . . . . . . . . . . . . .208-209
Halloween Glowing Ghosts . . . . . . . . . . . .210-214
Henry Hawk . . . . . . . . . . . . . . . . . . . . . . 215
Hippo . . . . . . . . . . . . . . . . . . . . . . . . . . . 216

# M

# N

# O

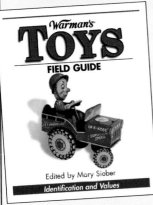